SCHOOLCRAFT COLLEGE LIBRARY

3 3013 00077 4855

 W9-CLF-828

GN
790
.I94
1975

Ivimy, John
The Sphinx and the
megaliths

BRADNER LIBRARY
SCHOOLCRAFT COLLEGE
LIVONIA, MICHIGAN 48152

The Sphinx
&
The Megaliths

The Sphinx
&
The Megaliths

John Ivimy

1817

HARPER & ROW, PUBLISHERS
New York, Evanston, San Francisco

913.031
GN 95
790
.I94
1975

THE SPHINX AND THE MEGALITHS. Copyright © 1975 by John Ivimy. All rights reserved. Printed in the United States of America. No part of this book may be used or reproduced in any manner whatsoever without written permission except in the case of brief quotations embodied in critical articles and reviews: For information address Harper & Row, Publishers, Inc., 10 East 53rd Street, New York, N. Y. 10022. Published simultaneously in Canada by Fitzhenry & Whiteside Limited, Toronto.

FIRST U.S. EDITION

Library of Congress Cataloging in Publication Data

Ivimy, John, 1911-
  The Sphinx and the megaliths.
  Includes bibliographical references and index.
  1. Megalithic monuments. 2. Stonehenge. 3. Cultus, Egyptian.   I.   Title.
GN790.I94   1975   930'.1   75-4270   ISBN 0-06-012152-1

75 76 77 78 79 10 9 8 7 6 5 4 3 2 1

TO MY WIFE

Acknowledgments

THE MAIN ideas propounded in this book are so widely at variance with those currently accepted in academic circles that I decided not to embarrass any professional archaeologist or Egyptologist by inviting comments on any part of it. For want of expert pre-publication criticism, therefore, it will not be surprising if the book is found to contain a higher than average number of errors and omissions. For any such I here apologise to the reader, and at the same time acknowledge in advance my debt to the critics and others who, I hope, will kindly point them out so that, should an occasion for correcting them arise, the text can be duly amended.

My thanks are due to Professor R. J. C. Atkinson of the Department of Archaeology, University College, Cardiff, for permission to quote extensively from his book *Stonehenge* and for the photograph of Stone no.36 that appears on page 86. I am particularly indebted to him for helpful advice on a number of specific points regarding the archaeology of Stonehenge. I thank also Professor Alexander Thom, Professor Emeritus of Engineering at the University of Oxford, for permission to reproduce text and diagrams from his book *Megalithic Sites In Britain*, and for his picture of the great menhir of Er Grah on page 62. Others to whom I am indebted for quotations and illustrations are Professor Charles H. Hapgood, lately of the University of New Hampshire; Dr Gerald S. Hawkins, astronomer and author of *Stonehenge Decoded*; Else Christie Kielland, artist and authoress of *Geometry In Egyptian Art*; and Dr André Pochan, physicist and mathematician, formerly professor at the French Lycée in Cairo and author of *L'Enigme de la Grande Pyramide*. I thank also their respective publishers whose names are cited in the notes.

I thank Mr Aubrey Burl and the Department of Evolution and Prehistory at the Kingston upon Hull College of Education for allowing me to use the drawings from which the map on page 60 was compiled, and the Department of the Environment for advice regarding the survey of Stonehenge.

To Mr Robert L. Merritt of Cleveland, Ohio, I am deeply grateful for his help and encouragement on many occasions and for introducing me to sources of information which I would otherwise have missed.

Finally, I am indebted to Mrs D. A. Turner, who lived for a while in Kalamata, for the story about the locomotive on page 99.

The following illustration sources are acknowledged with thanks:

1. Photo: Egyptian Tourist Information Centre; 5. Drawing by le Comte Begouen and l'abbé Breuil in *Manuel de Préhistoire Générale* by R. Furon (Payot, Paris, 1951); 7. Papyrus in the Bibliotheque Nationale, Paris. Photo: A. Giraudon; 8. Drawing by M. André Pochan in *L'Enigme de la Grand Pyramide* (Robert Laffont, Paris, 1971); 9. Funerary Papyrus *The Judgement of Osiris*, Louvre. Photo: A. Giraudon; 10. Drawings by W. B. Emery in *Archaic Egypt* (Pelican 1961), Penguin Books. Copyright, the Estate of Walter B. Emery, 1961; 11. From the painting by Ingres, Louvre. Photo: A. Giraudon; 14. From drawings by Mr. Aubrey Burl, Department of Evolution and Prehistory, Kingston upon Hull College of Education; 15. Photo: Professor A. Thom; 16. Photo: Cambridge University Collection; 17, 19, 20, 22, 34. Photos: Department of the Environment. Crown Copyright — reproduced with the permission of the Controller of Her Majesty's Stationery Office; 18. Photo: French Government Tourist Office; 21. Photo: Professor R. J. C. Atkinson; 23. Drawing by Dr. G. S. Hawkins in *Stonehenge Decoded* (Doubleday & Co. Inc., New York); 25. Radiograph by Kodak Ltd, London; 29. Drawing by Professor A. Thom in *Megalithic Sites in Britain* (The Clarendon Press, Oxford); 36. Hunefer Papyrus, British Museum; 37. Photo: Feature-Pix Colour Library; 38. Danish National Museum, Copenhagen; 39. The Ani Papyrus, British Museum; 40. Photo: The Mormon Church of Jesus Christ of Latter Day Saints.

Copyright is reserved in all of the above illustrations.

Contents

List of illustrations　　　　　　　　　　　　　　　xi
Preface　　　　　　　　　　　　　　　　　　　　1

PART ONE — THE SPHINX

1. Egypt of the Pharaohs ....　5
2. The Riddle of the Sphinx.....................　15
3. The Ancient Wisdom ....　42

PART TWO — THE MEGALITHS

4. The Mystery of the Megaliths ....　61
5. The Archaeology of Stonehenge ....　75
6. Inferences from Archaeology..................　83
7. Myths and Magic ....　93
8. Archaeologists and Astronomers...............　106
9. Arithmetic and Geometry ....　123
10. The Aubrey Holes...........................　139

PART THREE — THE STORY

11. The Founding of Stonehenge..................　152
12. The Message of the Megaliths.................　160
13. A Waxing and a Waning ....　171

PART FOUR — EPILOGUE

14. A Modern Parallel ....　183

Appendix 1.　Extracts from *Megalithic Sites in Britain* .　191
Appendix 2.　Extracts from *Geometry in Egyptian Art* .　193
Appendix 3.　The Geometry of the Aubrey Circle......　196
Index　　　　　　　　　　　　　　　　　　　　199

List of Illustrations

1.	The Sphinx	4
2.	The Nile Valley	6
3.	The Three Crowns of Egypt	8
4.	The Pyramids of Giza	12
5.	The Dancing Shaman of The Cave of Les Trois Frères, Pyrenees	18
6.	Eight principal Gods of the Egyptians	20
7.	A Procession of Gods	23
8.	The Obelisks of Heliopolis	24
9.	The Weighing of Souls	31
10.	Horus and Seth	32
11.	Oedipus and the Sphinx	35
12.	The Djed Column	36
13.	The Oronteus Finaeus map of 1532	58
14.	The principal Stone Rings in the British Isles	60
15.	Er Grah: Le Grand Menhir Brisé	62
16.	Aerial View of Stonehenge	64
17.	Sunrise over the Heel Stone	66
18.	The Standing Stones of Carnac	69
19.	Stonehenge	76
20.	Silbury Hill	84
21.	Stone 36, Stonehenge	86
22.	Avebury	97
23.	Astronomical Alignments at Stonehenge	108
24.	Logarithmic or *Phi* spiral	126
25.	Radiograph of *Nautilus pompilius*	127
26.	The proportions of the Great Pyramid	130
27.	Egyptian Measures and the Megalithic Yard	133
28.	Section through the Great Pyramid	134
29.	Egg-shaped Stone Ring	135
30.	Stonehenge I	141
31.	The Scale	142

32. The Foresight 143
33. Map of part of Wiltshire 145
34. Plan of Stonehenge 147
35. Seven pointed star 148
36. Shu and Tefnet 162
37. The Lions of Delos 170
38. The Gundestrup Cauldron 178
39. Detail of the Ani Papyrus 179
40. The Mormon Temple 188

Preface

ANCIENT RECORDS are unreliable guides to the quality of ancient thoughts. If, for instance, we were to maintain that the state of the knowledge of mathematics possessed by any given culture in antiquity was no more advanced than it is proved to have been by the surviving documentary evidence, we would have to draw the conclusion that some of the outstanding engineering feats of ancient peoples were no more than the occasional fluke successes of crude trial-and-error methods.

According to the available literary evidence, it was not until the second century AD that mathematical techniques were developed such as would have made it possible to plan and execute with precision the construction of a tunnel through a mountain by men digging from both ends simultaneously. If one were to accept that evidence as conclusive, one would have to draw the logical conclusion that the engineer who was employed by Polycrates (tyrant of Samos, about 540 BC), to bore an aqueduct 900 yards long through the hill of Kastro had an astonishing piece of good luck when, as has been shown by modern excavations, the centre lines of the tunnels bored from both ends proved to be only 2 feet out when they met in the middle.

It may be no coincidence that Polycrates was a friend of Amasis, king of Egypt, and that through the latter's good offices he had arranged some time previously for one of his subjects, a young man named Pythagoras who showed some aptitude with numbers, to be initiated into the Egyptian priesthood and to study their ancient lore. But whether it was Pythagoras himself or some Egyptian mathematician-priest who made the calculations for the tunnel, the important point is that the state of mathematical knowledge in the 6th century BC has been proved by modern archaeology to have been actually far in advance of what had previously been supposed.

A similar discovery, that people in Stone Age Britain in the second, and even the third, millennium BC knew more about mathematics and astronomy than anyone had thought possible,

1

has been made in the last decade as a result of scientific surveys of Stonehenge and other Megalithic sites. Our first concern in writing this book was to suggest answers to the question: How and whence did the builders acquire the knowledge and skills that they have thus been shown to have possessed? But our enquiry did not end after completing the presentation of the detailed evidence supporting our view that these people came from Egypt, the only civilized country then in existence within reasonable reach of Britain. A more profound question clamoured for an answer: *Why* were those skills and that knowledge applied in the way they were? What were the motives that drove the men of that far distant age in this remote island to the prodigious exertions that were needed to accomplish those astonishing feats of engineering virtuosity, and to execute them, moreover, with such precision that the length of the unit of measurement they used could be ascertained four thousand years later, correct to the nearest millimetre?

In putting forward our theory of the quest on which these people were engaged we enter a realm of pure speculation in which it is useless to turn to the scientist for enlightenment. For no true scientist will theorise in public on flimsy evidence or commit himself to say Yea or Nay to the reasonable speculations of others; and no evidence yet unearthed gives more than the faintest clue to the motives of the men who built the hundreds of stone rings that are still to be found dotted over the uplands from the south coast of Brittany to the north of Scotland and the Outer Hebrides.

Whilst, however, the Great Stones offer little hope that their purpose and meaning will ever become fully clear from their own evidence alone, nevertheless when they are considered against the background of their contemporary Bronze Age cultures in Egypt and the Middle East, and when the evidence of Greek historians is also taken into account, a pattern emerges that has enabled us to sketch the outline of a coherent story of Stonehenge from its foundation to its ultimate abandonment by the descendants of its founders nearly two thousand years later. We make no claim, however, that this is the only such story that could plausibly be told.

Among the many unorthodox ideas that the reader will find scattered throughout the book, perhaps the most startling will be found in the passages on religion where we discuss the attitudes of priests towards their natural environment and the place occupied therein by the gods they worshipped. Most accounts of the religions of ancient primitive societies are based, consciously or unconsciously, on knowledge derived by anthropologists of the religions of contemporary primitive societies which by good fortune still survive in remote corners of the globe. It is tacitly assumed that the relation between, say, a priest of Anu or Seth and his god in 3000 BC was analogous to that of a priest of an aboriginal Polynesian tribe and his god today.

This assumption fails to take into account a vital difference between the two kinds of society. The still extant primitive society is a socially static and genetically homogeneous unit that has remained essentially unchanged for centuries, and in which, therefore, there is little difference between the levels of intelligence of the priest or witch-doctor and the people he ministers to. On the other hand the societies that comprised the earliest civilizations in Asia and Africa were dynamic, developing cultures, often of mixed racial origins, in which there must have existed a powerful urge on the part of the cleverest men to improve their condition and to use their brains to set themselves above men of lower intelligence who were content merely to remain as they were. Situated at the growing-point of the tree of cultural evolution, those Bronze Age societies were engaged in an upward struggle towards ever higher and higher levels of civilization, whilst the present-day tribesmen of Polynesia or Brazil are happy just to perpetuate the culture level they reached when they branched off from the main stem, perhaps thousands of years ago.

No analogy from modern anthropological evidence can therefore be accepted by itself as a valid argument against a radical new interpretation of the role of priesthoods and religion in early civilized societies. Since there are no records, and none are ever likely to be found, to reveal the inner thoughts of the High Priest of Ra or the Priestess of Pythian Apollo as they offered sacrifices and prayers to their respective deities, it is only possible to speculate about what those thoughts may have been.

The test by which such speculation should be judged is not the same as that by which the validity of scientific theories is properly judged. The question to be asked is not: what solid evidence exists to prove that these ideas are right; but rather: does any solid evidence exist to prove them wrong, and if not, do they offer a sensible and coherent explanation of what would otherwise be a confused jumble of unrelated facts?

It is by this test that the author invites the reader to judge the story that is submitted in the last chapters of this book.

Part One The Sphinx

1 Egypt of the Pharaohs

THE HISTORY of sovereign pharaonic Egypt is divided symmetrically into three 'kingdoms' or long settled periods of ordered development, interrupted by two shorter intervals of disorder. The first of the settled periods was the thousand-year-long Old Kingdom (c. 3200-2200 BC), comprising the first six Dynasties of Pharaohs.[1] It began with the unification of the two warring states of Upper and Lower Egypt by Menes, the founder and first King of the First Dynasty, and it ended in a violent social revolution at the end of the Sixth Dynasty.

For the greater part of its long history the Old Kingdom may be described in broad terms as an enlightened autocracy that exercised a beneficent rule over a peace-loving and industrious people. It brought them up from a primitive state of tribalism to a prosperous and efficiently organised economy that proved itself capable of producing some of the greatest monuments of civilized man that the world has seen. But although the political system under which this remarkable result was achieved — a system that endured substantially unchanged for a thousand years — must rank as one of the outstanding inventions in the history of civil government, nothing whatsoever is known about the life of the man who invented it.

In Egyptian records the first King of the united Kingdom is variously referred to as 'Narmer' and 'Hor-aha', 'Menes' being his Greek name. The late Professor W. B. Emery thought it likely that Narmer was the name of a warrior who annexed the northern to the southern Kingdom by military conquest and who passed the succession to both Kingdoms to Hor-aha. In that case 'Menes' was the Greek name for Hor-aha, the true founder and organiser of the Egyptian nation who, like Augustus following in the wake of Julius Caesar's conquests, welded the two halves of his world together by political skill into a single organic whole.

One of the founder's first tasks would have been to define the boundaries of the administrative districts ('nomes') into which he

1. (opposite) The Great Sphinx

5

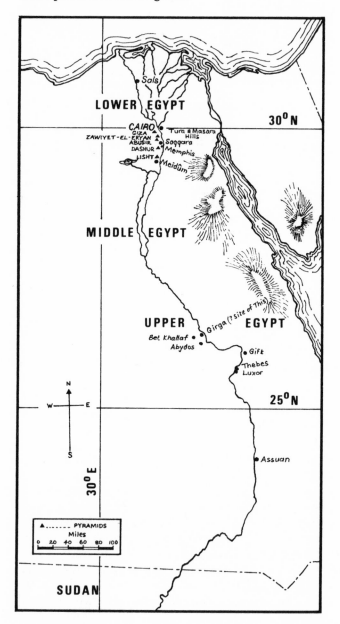

2. The Nile Valley

divided his Kingdom, and to appoint a governor ('nomarch') over each. Another was to build a capital for himself and his central government (known collectively as 'the pharaoh') and to define the relations and responsibilities of the nomarchs vis-à-vis the pharaoh. With tact and foresight he chose an ideal site for his capital, on the formerly disputed border between Upper and Lower Egypt. Here he founded the city of Memphis, near the modern village of Sakkara, on the west bank of the Nile just south of the apex of the Delta. According to Herodotus, Menes acquired the site by diverting an arm of the Nile by means of a dam — a colossal feat of engineering.

The chief splendour of Memphis was the great temple that Menes built there in honour of Ptah, patron god of the arts and sciences and of pharaonic government, and tutelary god of the city of Memphis itself. It may be presumed that a large part of the temple was occupied by a priestly college for the training of what today would be called the higher civil service — the priest-administrators and technicians who were to govern Egypt honestly and efficiently over the coming centuries. From the results achieved it is reasonable to conclude that, at any rate during the first four Dynasties, appointments in this civil service were not made haphazardly or by nepotism, but that candidates had to prove by a suitable objective test that they possessed an exceptionally high standard of intelligence.

Three principal tasks were entrusted to the nomarchs: the supervision of public works, including in particular the control of land irrigation by canals from the Nile; the collection of taxes, for which biennial censuses were taken; and the administration of justice. Menes laid down no written code of laws but enjoined his judges to judge according to 'ma'at' — an Egyptian word having no exact European equivalent but which signified a mixture of our notions of truth, order, and divine or 'natural' justice. In modern terms this would mean that the Egyptian judges of the Old Kingdom were not slaves to precedents or rigid rules of law, but had to judge each case as best they could in the light of their natural sense of justice and ordinary commonsense.

To give the people as a whole a sense of nationhood, of belonging no longer to one of two rival kingdoms but to the new united Kingdom, a new image or symbol was needed. This Menes devised in the shape of the *pschent* or double crown, in which he combined the white (gold) crown of Upper Egypt with the red (copper) crown of Lower Egypt in such a way that neither had precedence over the other. (In just the same way and for the same purpose King Henry VII combined the white rose of York with the red rose of Lancaster to make the double Tudor rose of his united England.)

3. The Three Crowns of Egypt. *A. The white crown of Upper Egypt. B. The red crown of Lower Egypt. C. The* Pschent *or double crown of the united Kingdom.*

So the master mind of its founder set the Egyptian nation on its long straight course of progress towards the achievement of domestic harmony and rational control of its environment. The middle centuries of the Old Kingdom were the Golden Age of Egyptian history. Sir Arnold Toynbee in his classic work *A Study of History* described it thus. 'The impetus which manifested itself first in the mastery of a peculiarly formidable physical environment — in the clearing, draining, and cultivation of the jungle-swamp that originally occupied the lower valley and the Delta of the Nile to the exclusion of Man — and which then displayed its increasing momentum in the precocious political unification of the Egyptiac World at the end of the so-called Predynastic Age, reached its climax in the stupendous material performances of the Fourth Dynasty. The Age of the Fourth and Fifth Dynasties was the zenith of Egyptiac history, by whatever criteria we measure the curve of its progress and decline. It was the zenith in the characteristic achievement of the Egyptiac Society: the co-ordination of human labour in great engineering enterprises ranging from the reclamation of swamps to the construction of the Pyramids. It was also the zenith in the spheres of political administration and of art. Even in the sphere of religion, where wisdom is proverbially born of suffering, the so-called 'Pyramid Texts' testify that this age likewise saw the creation, the collision, and the first stage in the interaction of the two religious movements — the worship of the Sun and the worship of Osiris — which came to their maturity after the Egyptiac Society had gone into its decline. The zenith was passed and the decline set in at the transition from the Fifth Dynasty to the Sixth.'[2]

In the realm of technical and administrative inventiveness it can be argued that the zenith occurred a little earlier, in the Third Dynasty. In the person of Imhotep, vizier of King Zoser, the first King of that Dynasty (c. 2750 BC), Egypt produced a many-sided genius whose like has rarely been seen in any age. Mathematician, architect, engineer, priest, physician, poet, and administrator, Imhotep left his mark in every field of endeavour. He it was who built the first of the Egyptian pyramids, the Step Pyramid of Sakkara (Ptah-Soker), reputed to be the first edifice ever built in stone. It stands to-day substantially intact amid the ruins of many pyramids built by lesser men at later dates. The American archaeologist G. A. Reisner described this building as 'a wonderful translation of the older brick architecture with wooden accessories into dressed limestone'. It revealed, he said, 'an astonishing mastery over the hard materials of the earth and an opulence in power without precedent in Egypt before this time. It shows the civilization of Egypt approaching its climax.'[3]

It was characteristic of Imhotep's genius that when faced with two seemingly insoluble problems he found one answer that solved both simultaneously. The first was a religious problem: how to save the body and soul of the pharaoh, in whom were personified the body and soul of the Egyptian nation, and preserve them to everlasting life. The second was the economic question how to deal with the problem of unemployment that was caused by the population increasing faster than the economy could expand to absorb it. The answer to both problems was the pyramid. On the one hand the design and construction of the pyramid were such that when the King died the sarcophagus containing his mummified body could rest in the rock-hewn sepulchre beneath it, safe from destruction by the elements for all eternity (the pyramid shape being chosen simply because it was more durable than any other); and on the other hand its size was such that building it would provide work directly for thousands of men for a decade or more and indirectly for tens of thousands more, and thus save them from the only alternative that lay open to them — death by starvation.

Thus guided by the genius of their inspired leader the Egyptian nation basked for centuries in the comfortable belief that they had overcome Death and found the secret of eternal national life. No wonder that later generations worshipped Imhotep as a god. Pharaoh after pharaoh followed Zoser's example, built his pyramid and went his predestined way, or so he thought, to join the sun god Ra in his boat of millions of years.

But Death was not so easily defeated. There is no record of the causes or the course of the Egyptian Revolution, but it is not hard to guess what may have happened. Complacent in their belief that their religious and economic problems had been solved for all time by Imhotep, the governments of the Fifth and Sixth Dynasties ignored the rumblings of the coming storm and continued blindly on the course that had been set by that divine master. A situation arose not unlike that of France under Louis XV and XVI or of Russia in the last days of the Czars. The cause of the rumblings was the intolerable burden of taxation on the peasants, which was aggravated by the spectacle of an ever growing army of priests and nobles for whose maintenance in indolent comfort the taxes were imposed. If taxes had been levied to meet, besides the annual costs of government, only the construction cost of the pyramid that was currently being built, and if the nobility and the churches had borne their fair shares of that cost, all might yet have been well. But every pyramid was endowed with a college of priests who were employed in singing hymns and saying prayers for the dead King's soul and in providing food, drink and comforts for his mummified body in perpetuity. The costs of the pyramid policy were thus cumulative. To meet them the level of taxation had continually to be raised; and the higher the level the greater was the dexterity shown by nobles and priests in evading their share of the burden. At length the common people could bear it no longer. They rose in their thousands, stormed the palaces and the mansions, slaughtered the priests and nobles and ransacked the tombs of the dead.

The revolution that overthrew the Sixth Dynasty was the prelude to a century or more of social unrest and political instability known as the First Intermediate Period. Out of it at length emerged the powerful Middle Kingdom Pharaohs of the 11th and 12th Dynasties (c. 2100-1780 BC). These kings established their capital at Thebes in Upper Egypt. Perhaps we should not call them kings but dictators, for not only in its revolutionary origin but in other ways also the Egyptian Middle Kingdom bore interesting resemblances to a modern fascist or communist dictatorship.

Its social policies were conspicuously oriented towards collectivist objectives, and by means of a vast bureaucracy supported by secret police it exercised a detailed control over the daily lives of its citizens. Its attitude to religion was also akin to that of communism. The cult of the obscure local god Amon of Thebes was cynically turned by atheist officials into a powerful state religion to exploit the people's simple faith and to harness it to the service of the State.

The Middle Kingdom government was a monolithic structure that must have seemed at the time to be indestructible. It was nevertheless suddenly and completely destroyed, not by an uprising from within but by invasion from without. The invaders were the Hyksos, or so-called 'Shepherd Kings', from Asia. Exactly who they were and whence they came has never been established with certainty, but it is generally accepted that they were semitic bedouin tribesmen from the eastern desert. How they were able without, apparently, any outstanding leader or formal organisation to descend on the Nile valley out of a blue sky, and without even fighting a battle, to overthrow the most powerful state in the world is one of the great mysteries of ancient history. One fact is clear from the record of the historian Manetho: that the Egyptian government system was obliterated and its functions usurped by foreigners without any effective resistance being put up either by the army or by the people. From this it may fairly be deduced either that the regime was so hated that the people were glad to see it go, or that three centuries of collectivist rule had so stifled individual initiative that when their officials were removed the people were incapable of thinking and acting for themselves.

The rule of the Hyksos, known as the Second Intermediate Period, lasted about two centuries. The foreigners were finally driven out by the Egyptian Ahmose I, founder of the New Kingdom or Empire (1567-1085 BC). The three Dynasties (18th to 20th) that comprised this period included many great pharaohs: Thutmose III, 'the Egyptian Napoleon' who carried the Empire's eastern frontier to the Euphrates; the powerful Queen Hatshepsut; the poet King Akhenaton who deposed the lying priests of Amon and substituted the monotheist cult of the sun's disc Aten; his boy heir Tutankhamen under whom the priests of Amon were restored to even greater power than before; and the most celebrated because the most vainglorious of all Egyptian pharaohs, Rameses II.

4. The Pyramids of Giza

The New Kingdom was a glorious and eventful period. It was also a time of tensions and strife, and it ended in divisions at home, declining influence abroad and eventual domination by foreign powers. Even at the peak of its imperial power and material prosperity the New Kingdom never matched the success of the enlightened administration of the Old Kingdom in securing the peaceful contentment of its people and their unhindered progress towards perfection in the achievement of their technical and artistic aspirations.

The Old Kingdom before it declined was indeed the Golden Age of Egyptian history. Its culminating achievement was the building of the three great pyramids of Giza, of which the biggest, and the oldest, is the Great Pyramid of Cheops (Khufu).

No building that has ever been or ever will be built can excite more wonder than the Great Pyramid. No records have come down from ancient Egypt to tell us authoritatively when, how, and why the Pyramid was built, nor what is the meaning of its mysterious passages and chambers. Such ancient writings as do still exist are merely legends. In modern times numerous surveys have been made of its external and internal dimensions, and hundreds of books and papers have been written propounding and refuting one theory after another; but those questions remain without convincing answers. A recent panoramic study of the many problems posed by the Pyramid[4] contains a bibliography of over 300 books. Not one of the many diverse theories that it summarises gives satisfactory answers to all the questions. Was the Pyramid built, as professional Egyptologists generally aver, to serve no other purpose than to be a Pharaoh's tomb, or was it also a public work for the relief of unemployment, or a temple for Isiac rites, or an astronomical observatory, or a calendar and record of astronomical and geodetic measurements, or a prophesy of the future destiny of mankind? Or was it all these things together — a marvellous consummation of men's endeavours to create what Nature herself delights in creating: one instrument to serve many purposes?

Until the truth has been definitely established every enquirer is free to assess the evidence in accordance with his natural predilections. In a later chapter, where we compare certain mathematical features of the Pyramid with those of Megalithic stone circles in Britain, we shall take advantage of this freedom to throw in yet one more idea as a contribution to the discussion.

The second pyramid in both age and magnitude is that of Cheops' son Chephren, and the third is attributed to Chephren's successor Mykerinos. It is believed to have been in Chephren's reign that there was carved out of the rock of the Giza plateau looking east over the Nile that massive symbol that guards the pyramids: the Great Sphinx.

Mysterious, enigmatic, inscrutable. Such epithets have been applied throughout history to the Egyptian Sphinx. The same epithets can be applied just as aptly to the Egyptian priests who carved the Sphinx and built the Pyramid. This is no coincidence. In the next chapter we shall try to show that the Sphinx's ambivalent form was a device invented by the priests of the Old Kingdom as a secret sign, understood only by the initiates, to symbolise the priesthood itself and its guardianship of the cosmic mysteries enshrined in the Pyramid to which they alone possessed the secret clues.

Notes on Chapter 1

1) The first two Dynasties are usually referred to nowadays as the 'Archaic period', the Old Kingdom proper being regarded as commencing with the Third Dynasty. But there was no break in the continuity of progress at that point, and for the sake of simplicity we prefer to keep the old nomenclature.

2) Arnold J. Toynbee, *A Study of History* (Oxford University Press, published under the auspices of the Royal Institute of International Affairs, Vol. 1, p. 136).

3) G. A. Reisner, *The Development of the Egyptian Tomb Down to the Association of Cheops* (Harvard University Press, Cambridge 1936).

4) Peter Tompkins, *Secrets of the Great Pyramid* (Harper & Row, New York 1971).

2 The Riddle of the Sphinx

ACCORDING to an inscription of the 18th Dynasty the Sphinx represents three gods in one: Harmakhis, the rising sun; Khepri, the sacred scarab that re-creates itself out of its own substance; and Atum the god-king who was the progenitor of the human race and who also symbolised the setting sun and the sun before its rising. The whole is thus a symbol of the resurrection, or the sun-like cycle of human birth, death, and rebirth.

But why was this particular form chosen — a recumbent figure with the body of a lion and the head of a man? So far from resembling a god, the Sphinx was the exact antithesis of the popular idea of divinity current among the mass of the Egyptian people at this time. Of the huge number of gods worshipped in the Old Kingdom the great majority had human bodies and animal heads. Not one resembled the Sphinx in having an animal body with a human head. Nor is there any evidence that the Sphinx was worshipped as other gods were or regarded like them as being capable of action and movement. Manifestly, it was a symbol rather than a deity.

Modern Egyptologists attribute a strictly functional purpose to the Sphinx's form. 'In Egyptian mythology', we are told, 'the lion often figures as the guardian of sacred places . . . In the form of the Sphinx, the lion retained the function of a sentinel, but was given the human features of the Sun-god Atum '.[1] The head is believed to be an idealised portrait of the pharaoh Chephren who was thus identified with the Sun god.

On this interpretation the purpose of this choice of form was simply to represent a divine sentinel on watchful guard over the tombs of the pharaohs in their pyramids. But the Egyptian priests were past masters in the arts of dissimulation and of expressing themselves cryptically in double meanings. It would be unsafe to assume that when one reasonable explanation of a sacred symbol has been found there is no need to look for a deeper hidden meaning. In the Sphinx, as in the Pyramid, the simple interpretation may be true, but it is unlikely to be the whole truth. The multiple initiation rites by which ancient

Egyptian priests, like modern Freemasons, progressed step by step from the lowest degree to the highest involved their introduction into successively more profound mysteries by an ordered sequence of revelation, like the peeling of an onion layer by layer from the plain exterior to the secret heart within. Where there is only one interpretation, and that an obvious one, there is no mystery.

Ancient legends tell of the Sphinx's Riddle. In the Greek myth of Oedipus we are even told what the Riddle was. The Sphinx asked: 'What is it that walks on four legs in the morning, on two at noon, and in the evening upon three?' The answer was 'a man', because as an infant he crawls on all fours, he walks upright in his prime, and he leans on a stick in his old age.

We have already suggested that the Egyptian priesthood was recruited with the aid of objective tests by which the most intelligent boys were selected for initiation into its secrets. Such tests would have been, in effect, the world's first civil service examinations. If the Sphinx symbolised the priestly administration, then the distant memory of those ancient examinations would account for the legend of the Sphinx's riddle.

In the provincial society of Boeotian Thebes where the Oedipus myth originated, the particular riddle associated with that myth could have provided an effective means of selecting the brightest youths for entry into the trainee grade of the Greek priesthood; but it would hardly have been a suitable test for the promotion of young priests into the higher ranks of the all-powerful Egyptian civil service. For that purpose there was need of a more discriminating intelligence test. Such a test, we suggest, might have been provided by the riddle of the Sphinx's own form.

To the mass of ordinary people the Sphinx would have appeared simply as a divine image not significantly different from many others. They would no more think of looking for a meaning in its hybrid form than they would ask themselves why their god Horus had the head of a hawk. But a discerning young man who had already served some years in the junior ranks of the priesthood and had seen something of the far-sighted wisdom and calm rationality of its higher direction might have sensed a connection between that central focus of high intelligence and the calm and watchful countenance of the Sphinx. Had such a man been asked in an examination to write what he thought the Sphinx might say in answer to the question: what are you? he might have written thus:

'I am the Great Sphinx, the Pharaoh, the priestly government of Egypt. My head is that of a man. It represents Intelligence. My body is that of a lion, the strongest of beasts. It represents Force. My body is recumbent but my head is held high. Head and body together represent Force in repose controlled by Intelligence. My eyes are open, my ears are listening, but my mouth is closed. My being is silent, watchful, and at peace. I am the ideal state, the perfect government, the royal priesthood of Egypt.'

The tradition of mystery, secrecy, and deception that characterised the Egyptian and other ancient priesthoods can be traced far back into the Old Stone Age when the priests were shamans or magicians acting the part of animal gods. On cave walls in France can still be seen pictures drawn more than 10,000 years ago showing such wizards wearing bears' or calves' masks, dancing or playing the pipes. The simple people who witnessed these performances did not know that there was a man like themselves, or more probably a boy, inside the mask. They did not look closely at the join between the mask and the body (in later times usually concealed by a wide collar of beads) because their critical faculties, such as they were, were numbed with awe in the presence of this fearsome creature performing 'miracles' — feats like making musical sounds come out of an empty reed, which to them were impossible and which therefore proved that the creature performing them was possessed of supernatural powers; in other words, he was a god.

For the shaman or priest the performance of a miracle was an act of magic: that is to say, it was an act of deception whereby he demonstrated that the masked boy was a god because of his supernatural powers and that he himself had the ability (which his audience did not have) to communicate with and influence the god. By this means he inspired the people with faith in his capacity to bring divine power to bear on the people's affairs, either favourably if they were good and obedient to his will, or unfavourably if they failed, for example, in their duty to provide the god with the sacrifices of meat and drink that he demanded of them.

For countless generations the livelihood and the power of priests depended on the people's faith in the capacity of their gods to perform miracles and in the ability of the priests to influence the gods. Whenever this faith declined, as it did when

5. The Dancing Shaman of
the Cave of Les Trois Frères,
Pyrenees. *Magdalenian culture of the Old Stone Age, c.
10-15,000 BC.*

religious technology (the art of magic as practised by the priests)
failed to keep a step or two ahead of current secular technology,
then the priests were in danger of having their deceptions
exposed. This, we suspect, is what happened in Egypt at the end
of the Old Kingdom and accounts at least in part for the disgrace
of religion and the ruin of the priesthoods in the Egyptian
revolution. But in the early centuries of the Old Kingdom the
danger of exposure was minimal for a peculiar reason: the fact
that Egyptian society at that time was a bi-racial society.

From recent archaeological discoveries it is now believed that
the seeds of civilization were not generated spontaneously in
Egypt but were imported into the country by a so-called
'dynastic' race of men who entered the Nile valley either direct
from the civilization in the Euphrates valley or from some
intermediate off-shoot of that civilization. They were men with
bigger frames and more capacious skulls than the indigenous
natives, and they would therefore have found it a simple matter

to dominate them both physically by the superior strength of their limbs and intellectually by their superior intelligence and knowledge. To deceive the natives by feats of magic and so impress them with their supernatural powers would have been an easy way of asserting their superiority.

Where the intellectual gap between rulers and ruled or between priests and their congregations is great there is always a temptation for the men on top to abuse their powers and to exploit the people underneath. If the dynastic race succumbed to this temptation in Egypt in the generations that preceded the Unification under Menes, that would account for the immense variety of animal-headed gods that originated there at that time. For religion in those circumstances is merely an easy source of income for its practitioners. The gods demanded sacrifices, and their demands had to be met by the people on pain of facing divine anger; and every natural affliction or calamity, as well as some that were not natural, was represented as an expression of that anger.

Religion therefore was business, and the big religions were big business. After the system of tribal law, with its tribal gods, had been replaced by territorial law the inception, expansion and demise of new religions became governed by economic laws similar to those that govern businesses in a free enterprise economy. Competition encouraged inventiveness in the field of magic and ruthlessness in the punishments that were inflicted in the name of the gods on those who withheld their offerings. So long as entry into the business of religion remained unrestricted, new deities continued to multiply. Every animal that was capable of inspiring fear or wonder was represented in one place or another as divine. Cat, dog, bull, cow, ram, ape, wolf, hawk, vulture, jackal, lion, lioness, frog, snake, crocodile, scorpion, beetle, hippopotamus — all these were deities that survived as such into the Dynastic era. No doubt there were others that were eliminated earlier by competition. Those that survived did not remain for long the gods of independent cults but gradually became merged into composite multi-deity religions for much the same reasons as those that cause businesses to merge in a modern capitalist economy. Mergers of churches, as of companies, tend to cut costs and increase revenues. Where a male animal cult was merged with a female it was easy to represent the two gods as having been married; in other cases other relations of kinship were usually invented to account for the union.

Anubis. Jackal god of
funeral rites

Osiris. Lord of the
Underworld and Judge of
the Dead

Ra-Harakhte. Sun god
and supreme Lord.

Horus. Falcon-headed
son of Osiris and Isis

6. Eight Principal Gods of the Egyptians

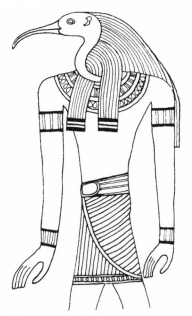

Thoth. Ibis god of wis-
dom and scribe to Osiris

Seth. Brother and enemy
of Osiris.

Ptah. Anthropomorphic
god of craftsmanship

Amon. The 'hidden one'
god of the Middle Kingdom.

In some temples the animal itself, for example a cat, would be kept in the sanctuary and shown to the worshippers from time to time as their god; but elsewhere the Old Stone Age practice of priests wearing animal masks was retained because the human body below the mask both enhanced the supernatural aspect of the deity and facilitated the performance of impressive feats of magic.

It is worthy of note that certain animals which one might expect would have become important gods, such as the elephant, the camel, and the giraffe, were worshipped either little or not at all. There are good technical reasons why this should be so. Clever though the Egyptian priests were, they could see no way of presenting plausible living images of human-bodied gods wearing masks of these animals' heads. The elephant's prehensile trunk and the long necks of the giraffe and the camel raised insuperable difficulties. It might be thought that equal difficulties would have been presented by small animals like snakes and insects, but wall paintings in tombs show how those problems were surmounted. In the case of beetles, large masks were made representing the whole insect, legs and all, moulded perhaps out of papier-maché and attached to a broad collar that fitted over the shoulders. Serpent gods were shown with just the snakes' heads protruding from a hood in which the man's head was concealed.

The animal cults flourished chiefly in the backward regions of Upper Egypt. In the Nile Delta they tended to be overlaid with a layer of more sophisticated beliefs which had reached Egypt by sea from Syria and the East. These included the worship of Ishtar, goddess of love (whose name became Isis in Egyptian) and the cult of the sun god Ra. It used to be thought that Osiris, the husband of Isis, was originally a King of a Lower Egyptian nome with its capital at Busiris where his worship was centred in Dynastic times. But Osiris is always represented in art as wearing the crown of Upper Egypt, and it has now been established that he was not the original god of Busiris but that he supplanted an earlier god there. His place of origin must therefore be looked for elsewhere. The most sacred temple of Osiris was at Abydos in Upper Egypt, and it is reasonable to infer that his cult originated in that region. In that case the identification of Osiris' wife with the goddess Isis must have occurred as the result of one of those merger processes just described.

7. An Egyptian Religious Tableau. *Four animal-headed gods carry the sun god Ra-Harakhte on his course (left) while others greet the rising sun and worship the scarab god Khepri (right)*

Both of the two great dominant religions of the Old Kingdom that are referred to in the extract from Toynbee's book quoted in the previous chapter, namely the sun cult of Ra and the worship of Osiris, are now believed to be considerably older than the Unification. The priests of Ra were highly intelligent men, famed throughout antiquity for the vast extent of their learning. The centre of their cult was Heliopolis, 'Sun-City' (now a suburb of Cairo), known to the Egyptians themselves as 'On'. Like all ancient priesthoods they were secretive about their activities, so we know little or nothing about what took place within the precincts of their temple. It may be doubted whether the lost works of the historian Manetho, a learned priest of Heliopolis who wrote in Greek in the third century BC, would have told us much more if they had survived. But the following passage from the work of the Arab chronicler Maqrizi of the 14th century AD is relevant to our present thesis.

> "Ain Shams is the temple of the Sun at Heliopolis where there stand two columns so marvellous that one has never seen anything more beautiful, nor even anything that approaches them. They are about 50 cubits (26.2 metres)

23

high and they rest on the surface of the ground . . . The points of their summits are made of copper . . . At the moment when the Sun enters the First Point of Capricorn, that is to say on the shortest day of the year, it reaches the southernmost of the two obelisks and crowns its summit; and when it reaches the First Point of Cancer, that is to say on the longest day of the year, it touches the northernmost obelisk and crowns its summit. These two obelisks thus form the two extreme points of the solar swing and the equinoctial line passes exactly between them . . ."[2]

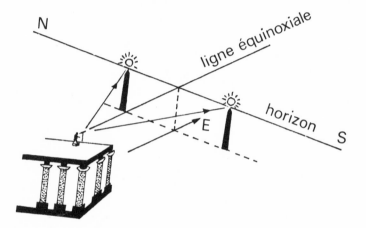

8. The Obelisks of Heliopolis

The evidence of the obelisks re-inforces the massive evidence already contained in the pyramids that the priests of Ra were no mean astronomers. It is safe to assume that they spent more time in observing the motions of the sun and in making predictions based on accurate measurements of its risings and settings than in offering sacrifices to it as a god, or praising it in hymns and imploring it to continue for ever to shed its beneficent rays on human kind. In other words, the temple of the Sun god at Heliopolis, although it was represented to the uninitiated as a place of religious worship, was in reality an astronomical observatory designed and equipped by scientists for essentially scientific purposes. Those Egyptian priests knew just as surely as we know today that the sun they pretended to worship was not the master but the robot slave of the laws of Nature.

Heliopolis was situated on the east bank of the Nile some 20 miles north of Memphis, which was on the west bank. Here the priests of Ra were far enough away from the capital to be able to pursue their studies independently of the administration but near enough to exercise an important influence on the religious education and beliefs of the King. At an early date in the Old Kingdom, probably shortly after the capital was moved from Abydos to Memphis at the end of the Second Dynasty, the image of Ra was superimposed on that of the falcon god Horus with whom the kings of both Kingdoms had been identified before the Unification, and thereafter the Pharaoh was represented as the son of the composite god Ra-Harakhte, depicted as a falcon with the solar disk on his head.

Now Ra and Horus were two gods of such very different characters and origins that it is hard to see how any merger between their respective priesthoods such as is implied by the union of their symbols could have been contemplated. Here then, is a problem that calls for investigation. What was the story behind Ra-Harakhte that made that union possible?

Horus was the second person of the holy trinity of the Osirian religion. This consisted of Osiris the father, Horus the son, and Thoth the god of wisdom and communication. Closely associated with this trinity were Isis or Hathor, wife and sister of Osiris and mother of Horus, her sister Nephthys, and the jackal-headed Anubis, son of Nephthys and god of funerals who conducted the souls of the dead to the judgement hall below. The second and third persons of the trinity, Horus and Thoth, were both bird-headed gods, the first a falcon and the second an ibis.

According to one version of the popular myth, Osiris was a tall dark man who came with Isis from a far country and taught the people the arts of civilization. He carried a sceptre, and they made him their king. He showed them how to plough and irrigate the soil, to measure the land and the seasons of the year, to lay out and build towns, to heal the sick, to make music, and many other arts, while Isis taught them how to cook and weave and sow, and other feminine skills. Osiris and Isis entered the Nile valley high up the river near the modern town of Luxor, and there they founded the city of Thebes, which became the capital of the Kingdom of Upper Egypt.

Osiris was the first King of Upper Egypt, but he did not reign for ever in peace. Twice he was killed by his wicked brother Seth who was jealous of his power. On the first occasion Seth shut him up in a box and sent him to drift down the Nile out to sea. The second time, he cut the king's body into pieces and buried them in different places all over Egypt. On each occasion Osiris was brought back to life by the devotion and magic powers of Isis. After the second murder, Horus, now grown up, avenged his father's death by defeating Seth in a long and bloody battle. Horus then reigned in his father's place while Osiris descended to the underworld to become judge to the dead.

Throughout Egyptian history Osiris was feared and worshipped as the perfectly just judge before whom every man and woman had to stand at death to receive sentence of the punishments and rewards that were due to them for their deeds in life.

Sir James Frazer in his monumental work on mythology, *The Golden Bough*, identified Osiris with the primitive corn-god or god of crop fertility. The story of Osiris' resurrection was, he said, intimately connected with the annual revival of vegetation; from that story the Egyptians derived their own hope of life after death. 'In laying their dead in the grave they committed them to his keeping who could raise them from the dust to life eternal, even as he caused the seed to spring from the ground. Of that faith the corn-stuffed effigies of Osiris found in Egyptian tombs furnish an eloquent and unequivocal testimony. They were at once an emblem and an instrument of resurrection. Thus from the sprouting of the grain the ancient Egyptians drew an augury of human immortality.'[3]

Modern scholarship has added considerably to our knowledge since Frazer's day. The late Professor W. B. Emery said that the Osirian cult, 'although having characteristics of nature worship, was primarily the worship of dead Kingship, and the myth of Osiris seems to be an echo of long-forgotten events which actually took place.'[4]

On this interpretation it is reasonable to identify the legendary King Osiris with the original pioneer of the infiltrating movement of settlers of the 'dynastic' race into the Nile valley from the east. Remains have been found of a highly developed civilization in the Euphrates valley that had connections with territories as far afield as central India and perhaps China, and whose roots went back many centuries before the Flood obliterated it some time in the fourth millennium BC. We may thus picture Osiris as a sort of prototype of Dr. Livingstone, an explorer and missionary from a high civilization who came striding through the jungle with a medicine chest on his back and a measuring rod (sceptre) in his hand, intent on bringing enlightenment to the benighted tribes of the dark continent.

That Osiris' motives were largely religious may be inferred from the legend itself. He was a just man, and he taught the natives that justice was eternal: evil deeds that went unpunished in this life would be punished in the next, and good deeds rewarded. This can be recognised to-day as the doctrine of *karma* that lies at the root of the Hindu religion, the oldest religion in the world, whence it was inherited by Buddhism. It may be described as the doctrine of 'psychogenic evolution' according to which the present state of every sentient being is determined by the quality of its own past actions, including actions in past lives. The effects of those actions manifest themselves automatically, for better or for worse, in the body and in the mind through the continuous cycle of birth, death, and rebirth, or perpetual reincarnation.

The lessons that were drawn from this Hindu doctrine by the lamas of Tibet are incorporated in the *Bardo Thodol* or *Tibetan Book of the Dead*. This is a treatise based essentially on the Occult Sciences of the Yoga Philosophy and constitutes 'an epitomized exposition of the cardinal doctrines of the *Mahayana* School of Buddhism'.[5] It bears such a remarkable resemblance to the Egyptian *Book of the Dead* as to suggest that there was some ultimate cultural relationship between the two. The Tibetan book was compiled by Padma Sambhava, 'the Precious Guru', founder of Tibetan Lamaism, who had been a Professor of Yoga in the Buddhist University of Nalanda in India in the 8th century AD; but much of its contents is known to be many centuries older, being pre-Buddhist in origin. The Egyptian book was presumably the work of priests of the Osirian religion and dates back to the Old Kingdom.

The similarity between the two books is particularly noticeable in regard to their doctrines of the Judgement and in the funeral rites they prescribe for the purpose of assisting the deceased to pass successfully through his ordeal. Both treatises are, in effect, 'nothing more than guide-books for the traveller in the realm beyond death.'[6]

The conclusion that Egyptian and Indian beliefs and rituals stemmed from a common origin is consistent with the widely held 'diffusionist' theory that civilization began with an explosion of ideas in the Euphrates valley and spread outwards from there.[7] The Biblical story of Adam and Eve in the Garden of Eden may well be a distant echo of that first civilization, dating back perhaps as far as the fifth millennium BC. In that case Adam, the 'first man' of the Book of Genesis, would be the same as Atum, the god-king and 'first man' of the Egyptian myth whose image, as we have seen, is supposed to be incorporated in the head of the Great Sphinx as symbolic of resurrection from death.

The earliest known civilizations occupied four river valleys: the Euphrates, the Nile, the Indus, and the Yellow River. There is evidence that all four were governed by ruling castes of mathematicians, for geodesy and astronomy figured prominently among their activities. It is reasonable to infer that 'Adam' or 'Atum' was the name by which the first king and founder of the first civilization was known, and that he was the mathematical genius who discovered the principle of trigonometry and thereby made possible the development of the three basic techniques of civilization: land survey, architecture, and engineering. All these techniques depend on the art of drawing to scale; and drawing to scale depends in turn on knowledge of the geometrical properties of triangles. The drama of civilization could never have begun if the stage had not first been lit for it by a mathematician.[8]

The precise meaning of the name 'Atum' in Egyptian is not certain, but it appears to be connected with the idea of 'completion' or 'perfection'. It would thus be a suitable name for a newly-born race of mathematicians to apply to their famous progenitor whose birth marked the culminating point in the evolution of the human intellect.

The connection between Atum and the concept of re-birth or resurrection could have arisen from the founder having also taught, like the mathematician Pythagoras, the doctrine of re-incarnation. That doctrine, with its concomitant idea of after-life justice, or *karma*, would then naturally have spread abroad, along with the technological ideas of the growing civilization, by explorers and missionaries such as we imagine the legendary Osiris to have been; and this would account for the similarity between the Egyptian and the Indian religious beliefs and practices.

Be that as it may, what concerns us here is that the worship of Osiris in Egypt was founded on belief in the re-incarnation of souls. According to that belief, only the souls of very good and perfect men, like Atum himself or the Pharaohs (as they were believed to be) and those of the very wicked, did not return to live again — the former because they had no need to perfect themselves farther and could therefore join the Sun god forthwith in his boat of millions of years, and the latter because they would be torn to pieces by wild beasts as soon as they left the Judgement hall.

In Classical times Osiris was identified with Dionysus (Bacchus) of Greek (and Roman) mythology — the god of wine and vegetation who descended into Hades and rose again from that realm of the dead. It is possible that the myth of the resurrection of Osiris originated, as Frazer maintained, in the same way as the story of the resurrection of Dionysus, namely in simple observations of the annual renewal of vegetable life. But if Osiris was a man who brought with him from the East the doctrine of *karma* to teach it to the natives of Africa, then the myth of his re-birth was more probably fastened onto his memory posthumously by his own offspring, the priests of the religion he founded, in an endeavour to fulfil his mission. Hence their representation of Osiris as ultimately remaining in the underworld as the stern judge of the dead, in contrast to Dionysus who, after his return from Hades, was lifted up to Mount Olympus. There, so far from concerning himself with the dead, the Greek god's main function was to promote the enjoyment of strictly carnal pleasures by mortals who were still very much alive on Earth.

Here, then, is the answer to our question. It is in the doctrine of reincarnation that we find the common denominator that linked the cult of Osiris with that of Ra and enabled the priests of Ra to accept Osiris' falcon-headed son Horus as being identical with the Sun god. Where the priests of Osiris pointed to the corn and the trees as evidence of the cosmic cycle of re-birth, the astronomer-priests of Ra pointed to the daily and yearly motions of the heavenly bodies which descended below the horizon in the west only to rise again later with renewed splendour in the east. But while other men are subject to this cycle, the divine Pharaoh, they said, was an exception. Like the circumpolar stars which never set, the souls of the Pharaohs remained continually alive and travelled for ever with the Sun god in his boat of millions of years.

We have no evidence to show that the priests of Ra believed in *karma*, nor, if they did, can we be certain what was the source of their belief. What can be said is, first, that belief in an automatic

29

system of justice would have been perfectly consistent with the scientific approach to cosmology that was adopted by this erudite order; and secondly that the founders of the order were more than likely to have been men of the dynastic race, in which case the probability is that they or their forebears came from Asia. This would explain the affinity between the priests of Ra at Heliopolis and the priests of Osiris at Abydos which led to the invention, by agreement between them on the Unification of the two Kingdoms, of the composite god Ra-Harakhte and his proclamation as the supreme tutelary deity of the Egyptian Pharaoh.

The Osirian religion, we have suggested, owed its origin to the teaching of Osiris himself, the pioneer missionary and first King of Upper Egypt, whose progeny carried on as priests his work of educating the natives. The esoteric doctrine of *karma* would have been handed down from generation to generation within the priesthood, but in its pure form it would have been far beyond the comprehension of the simple natives who were then inhabiting the Nile valley. For them the substance of the doctrine, as it affected their lives, had to be presented in a form they could understand. So, finding that they were wont to worship animal-headed gods, the missionary invented for them two new gods in the form of birds: Horus, the falcon, to punish the wicked in the next life, and Thoth, the ibis, to dispense rewards to the good. Birds were chosen in preference to beasts because their ability to fly was an apparently super-natural power that gave them divine significance.

It was the fear of Horus with the hawk's all-seeing eye and cruel beak that kept the natives in good disciplinary order. And since discipline was the most important product of religion from the point of view of the priests who administered the government, it was the image of Horus that was chosen to be the Pharaoh's personal emblem. Thoth, on the other hand, was a kindly god who was made the main instrument of Osiris' educational policy. He became in due course the god of children. The ibis form was chosen to symbolise the art of learning; for learning consists in picking tiny scraps of knowledge out of the muddy environment of everyday life and arranging them in the mind so as to produce composite ideas of truth and beauty, just as the ibis picks tiny insects out of the mud of the Nile with its long pointed beak and turns them into the beauty of its own feathered body.

Anubis the jackal god was not, we suggest, included in the

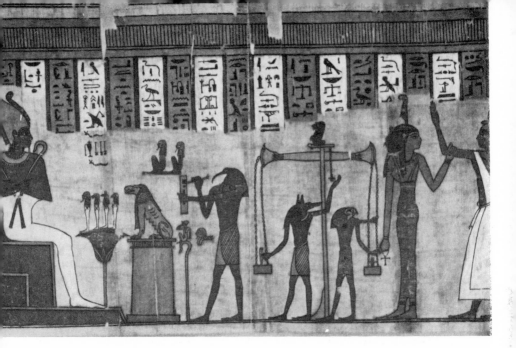

9. The Weighing of Souls. *Anubis and Horus operate the scales; Thoth records the weight; and Osiris delivers judgement*

original Osirian pantheon. He was more likely the local god of a tribe that was early converted to the Osirian faith. The choice of two birds as the original supporters of the father god was an important distinguishing mark of the religion. It was symbolised in typically Egyptian style in the conventional representations of Osiris whose headdress is the crown of Upper Egypt flanked on either side by a feather. In one hand the judge of the dead carries a hook, representing incentive rewards with which he pulled men forward from in front, and in the other a flail, representing deterrent punishments, with which he drove them from behind.[9] To make it clear that *karma* was a completely automatic system, depending on the deeds of the dead man himself and not on the arbitrary decision of the judge, the souls were represented as diminutive human beings that were weighed in scales by Anubis, the weight of the soul being balanced against a feather. The scales declared the dead man innocent or guilty; the judge pronounced the sentence.

New gods were invented and introduced into Egyptian society not only for religious purposes or for the purpose of commercial exploitation but also for political reasons. The worship of Ptah, the god of Memphis and of the arts and crafts, seems to be a clear example of a political religion, in this case invented by

Menes himself when he founded the city. Ptah was the ideal of the practical and industrious technician that Menes wanted his people to emulate in the new age of advanced technology inaugurated by his reign. In much the same way Caesar Augustus invented the goddess *Roma* and built temples to her in remote parts of his empire so that the people might emulate the virtues of the Romans and accept more peacefully the burdens and the benefits of Roman rule.

Perhaps the most striking example of Egyptian theological inventiveness is the animal god Seth. The Osirian myth in which Seth, the murderer of Osiris, fought with Horus and was finally conquered but not slain by him seems to echo the memory of a religious war that took place during the Second Dynasty. Archaeologists have found that at one time Seth actually displaced Horus as the royal deity, but under Kha-Sekhemui, the last king of the Second Dynasty, peace was established between the warring sects. This was probably the result of a personal effort of conciliation made by the Pharaoh, who commemorated his success by incorporating the images of both the gods in his emblem and taking a name meaning 'The Two Gods in Him are at Peace'.

10. Horus and Seth. *Three Pharaonic 'labels' of successive Kings of the Second Dynasty.*

The image of Seth is that of a dog-like animal with a long curved snout, tall erect square-topped ears and a forked tail. He has been variously identified with an ant-eater, an okapi, and even a donkey, but none of these animals fits the description.

The answer to the puzzle is to be found, we suggest, in the nature of the struggle between the Sethites and the Osirians. Whereas nowadays disputes between different religious denominations arise from differences of belief, in those far-off times in Egypt such disputes regarding the nature of the deity could not arise because the gods of both sides were plainly visible. Horus and Seth could be observed daily at the temple ceremonies in the shape of masked boys eating and drinking the sacrifices offered by the people and served up by the priests. The only question for dispute was which of several rival gods had the stronger claim to receive the suppliant's sacrifice.

At first there was little to choose between the claims of rival animal gods, and people's religions were determined by their tribal ancestry. But this balance was upset by the spread of the Osirians' doctrine that their feathered gods Horus and Thoth had power to dispense punishments and rewards after death. By thus carrying the religious conflict into the new dimension of the after-life the priests of Osiris gained a decisive advantage. Brandishing, as it were, the all-seeing eye of Horus as their new unbeatable weapon they threatened to reduce the priests of the furred animal gods to a state of impotence.

We must suppose that many of those priests were unscrupulous members of the dynastic race whose concern was to awe the natives by feats of magic in order to exploit them for their own advantage. Seeing their livelihoods threatened, they decided to halt the spread of the Osirian cult by opposing it with the image of a new animal god — or a new image of an old god — armed with *two* unbeatable weapons each as powerful as the eye of Horus. The new image was that of Seth, and the weapons were his ears and his nose. The eye of Horus, the Sethite priests pointed out, could not see what men did in the privacy of their own homes behind closed doors, nor could it penetrate the darkness of night. But Seth had tall alert ears and a long flexible nose. With his nose he could trace a thief in the night or sniff out any meat that was being hidden from him; and when people whispered together in secret his all-hearing ears would be listening at the door.

Nor was Seth less well armed than Horus for inflicting punishments. Against the latter's sharp talons and cruel beak he possessed a forked tail with a poisoned sting — a cross between the sting of a scorpion and the forked tongue of a cobra. A fierce set of teeth might have been more frightening, but it was not possible to represent it simultaneously with the sensitive snout; and the forked tail had the advantage that its effects were easier to simulate. A poisoned blade twice plunged by a masked priest into the throat of a Horus-worshipper while he slept would leave unmistakable evidence of Seth's vengeance, and to anyone who might be wavering in his allegiance would serve as a salutary reminder as to where his true interest lay. Truly, Seth was a god more to be feared than Horus.

It may be wondered why, when a religious conflict of this nature developed and spread to such an extent that the whole land was divided into warring factions, the priests on one side did not expose the deceptions of the enemy in order to alienate the bulk of his supporters. The reason is that leaders of both sides were equally vulnerable to such a manoeuvre. It was in their common interest that complete secrecy be maintained regarding the several ways in which priests deceived their congregations. That is why the utmost importance was attached to the initiation rites into the priesthoods of all ancient religions, when the most solemn vows were taken accompanied by the infliction of excruciating pain. No one who had stood that pain in order to learn the secrets of the priesthood was likely to give them away. Whatever differences divided them, even to the point of war, all priesthoods stood together in united condemnation of any of their numbers who might be tempted to divulge their secrets; for the exposure of one could lead to the downfall of all. Even as late as the classical period of Greek history not only renegade initiates but innocent parties who happened by accident to learn a religious secret were ruthlessly put to death.

'Pitiless' is an epithet commonly applied to the Sphinx. No priesthood ever showed mercy to one who might expose its secrets. Herein lies the significance of the Sphinx's riddle; for that riddle served two purposes. The first, already described, was to facilitate the selection of the most intelligent youths for entry into the priesthood, which was also the civil service. The second was more important. It was to ensure that no boy who was clever enough to guess the riddle was allowed to remain outside. In Egypt, anyone who could interpret the meaning of the man-headed lion would one day be able to penetrate the disguise of the beast- and bird-headed men, and then the whole fabric of the religious life of the nation would be imperilled. Intelligence had to be enlisted exclusively on the side of the gods.

The sphinx that figured in the mythology of Bronze Age Greece was represented as female, instead of male, with the head and bust of a woman. This suggests that religion in the Minoan and Mycenaean cultures was run by women. There is, indeed, other evidence to support the view that priestesses were more powerful that priests in the Bronze Age church of the

Olympian gods. But those priestesses were not always successful in keeping their secrets intact.

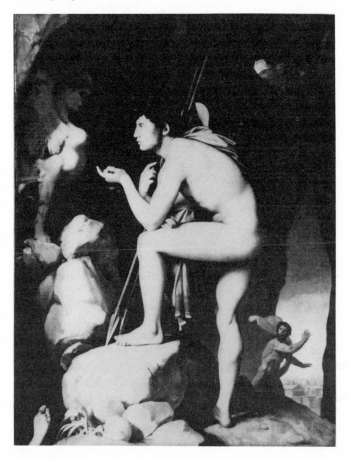

11. Oedipus and the Sphinx. *From the painting by Ingres.*

According to the legend, there was a Sphinx in Boeotian Thebes who sat on a rock outside the town and asked every Theban passer-by a riddle. Those who could not answer the riddle she strangled. One day Oedipus, the younger son, or so he believed, of Polybus and Periboea, king and queen of Corinth, came to Thebes and proclaimed the answer to the Sphinx's riddle. The Sphinx thereupon threw herself down from her rock and was killed, while Oedipus was made King of Thebes and married Jocasta, widow of the late King Laius whom he had himself unwittingly killed in a quarrel on the highway on his way to Thebes.

By reading 'priesthood' for 'Sphinx' this legend can be given a sensible historical meaning, as follows. Built on a rocky hill outside Thebes there was a great abbey which was used by the church of the Olympian gods as a seminary or training college for student priestesses and priests. The abbey, like the church as a whole, was governed by a woman. Using the riddle as an intelligence test, the abbess recruited into her college all the more intelligent girls and boys of Thebes. The less intelligent remainder of the population were held in a stranglehold of ignorance whilst heavy taxes were exacted from them to satisfy the material needs of the college.[10]

Oedipus was a violent and ambitious iconoclast who hated the priesthood, perhaps because he had failed their examination. Unable to guess the riddle, he extorted the answer from a priestess by threats of force or pretence of love, and then proclaimed it to the world. He then claimed the kingship of Thebes which he obtained by right of conquest as the slayer of Laius, and with it the automatic right to marry the late king's widow Jocasta. With an armed force he then attacked the seminary, slew the abbess and all the inmates, and razed the building to the ground.

But this was not the end of the story. Unknown to Oedipus, the Theban Sphinx had a mother. That mother now took a terrible revenge for her daughter's death. The High Priestess of the temple of Apollo at Delphi, sacred headquarters of the church of the Olympian gods in mainland Greece, contrived a diabolically cunning plot to bring the strong man down.

She waited some twenty years until Oedipus' father, the king of Corinth, died. Then, when Thebes was being ravaged by an epidemic, she instructed Queen Jocasta, who had been initiated as a priestess of Apollo, to persuade Oedipus to send a mission to the Delphic oracle to enquire the cause. The oracle told the Thebans that the plague would not cease until their city had rid itself of the cause of its pollution, namely the presence of a man who had killed his father and incestuously married his mother. Oedipus accepted the oracle, pronounced a curse on the unknown polluter and sentenced him to perpetual exile.

It was then revealed that the accursed man was none other than Oedipus himself. Jocasta pretended to recall that she and King Laius had had a boy baby which they had exposed on a hillside after they had been warned by the oracle that he, Laius, was destined to be killed by his own son. An old shepherd was suborned to tell how he had found the child and taken him to Corinth; Periboea, dowager queen of Corinth and, like Jocasta, a priestess under orders from Delphi, confirmed the shepherd's story and told how the baby had been taken in and brought up by her and her husband as their own son, Oedipus. (A priestess's vows of obedience to her church claimed absolute precedence over even the closest ties of marriage or motherhood.)

The unhappy Oedipus was overwhelmed by this unimpeachable evidence of his guilt. In an agony of remorse he took a brooch from Jocasta's dress and plunged the pin into both his eyes. Jocasta, her mind unhinged by the sight of that appalling deed, and tortured by the guilty knowledge of her own responsibility for it — a guilt that she could never confess — hanged herself. Oedipus bowed to the sentence he had passed on himself, left Thebes, and spent the rest of his days as a blind beggar in exile whose only comfort lay in the faithful support of his loving daughter Antigone.

So the Sphinx had her revenge — and more. For no genuine prophecy that was ever uttered by the Delphic priestesses earned so much profit for the oracle, because none brought it such world-wide renown for accurate long-range prediction, as was deceitfully obtained for it by the myth of Oedipus. But it was a hard-won victory for Intelligence over Force — one of the last to be won before darkness fell again and Force rose once more triumphant over Intelligence.

Notes on Chapter 2

1) I. E. S. Edwards, *The Pyramids of Egypt* (Penguin Books, London 1947).

2) Quoted by Monsieur André Pochan in *L'Enigme de la Grande Pyramide* (Robert Laffont, Paris, 1971).

3) Sir James G. Frazer, *The Golden Bough* (Macmillan, 1929. p. 381, abridged edition).

4) W. B. Emery, *Archaic Egypt* (Penguin Books, London 1961, p. 122).

5) Introduction to *The Tibetan Book of the Dead*, ed. W. Y. Evans-Wentz (Oxford University Press, New York).

6) Ibid.

7) See, for example, *The Makers of Civilisation* by Dr. L. A. Waddell (Luzac & Co., London, 1929) and *The Birth of Civilisation in*

the Near East by Professor Henry Frankfort (Williams & Norgate, London, 1951).

8) Comparison may be made with the explosion of ideas that followed the invention of the Infinitesimal Calculus by Newton and Leibnitz in the 17th century. That invention made possible the development of advanced techniques in architecture and engineering which paved the way for the Industrial Revolution of the 19th century.

9) A more usual view is that these emblems symbolise the two branches of agriculture — a threshing flail, standing for the cultivation of plants, and a shepherd's crook for animal husbandry. It seems to us much less likely that the artists who depicted Osiris in the exercise of his supreme function as Judge of the Underworld would have represented him as god of agriculture than as carrying the symbols of his divine power to dispense rewards and punishments to men after death.

In accepting the view that the hook or crook symbolises incentive rewards we may perhaps find an explanation of its curious striped appearance. It is nearly always shown made up of a large number of segments of alternate blue and gold. It is unlikely that this was just a piece of meaningless ornamentation, for the Egyptians never included superfluous ornaments in their religious art. Every detail was significant. The fact that in the vast majority of representations the hook (and sometimes, by analogy, the flail as well) was given this segmented appearance shows that the segmentation had a symbolic meaning.

We believe that in its oldest or original version the mathematical doctrine of *karma* offered the individual the prospect of attaining perfection by his own efforts in successive lives with the hope that, having attained it, he would enjoy immortal bliss in a perpetual series of perfect incarnations. Our suggestion is that in the Osirian insignia gold stands for the physical life on earth and blue for the spiritual existence in heaven. Then in the hook composed of alternate segments of gold and lapis lazuli the Supreme Judge (with whom the Pharaohs became identified after their death) is shown holding in his hand the ultimate incentive: the promise of life after blissful life of pleasure and happiness on earth alternating with periods of spiritual peace and regeneration in heaven.

A parallel interpretation can be applied to another favourite symbol of the Egyptian priests: the so-called *djed* column (Figure 12). The commonly accepted interpretation is that the *djed* represents the spinal column of Osiris and the source of the Fire of Life. We suggest it also had a more profound meaning revealed only to the highest initiates. For them it symbolised the whole process of psychogenic evolution. Life begins at the base of the column in micro-organisms which presently coagulate into multi-celled species. It then works its way up the evolutionary ladder through the forms of fishes, reptiles, and

12. 'Djed' Column. *The column is surmounted by the* ankh *with hands touching the solar disc.*

mammals, to man. The various steps are represented by the horizontal bars on the lower part of the *djed*. The appearance, near the top, of two arms holding the hook and the flail signifies the point where man first 'ate of the fruit of the tree of the knowledge of good and evil' and became a moral being. Below this point he was an animal motivated by biological desires and fears; above it he is possessed of self-control, or the power to over-ride those urges by rational decisions taken in the light of higher considerations, including the prospect of rewards and punishments in future lives. The series of horizontal platforms at the top of the column represents a series of human incarnations making continued upward progress. The platforms are broad to show the life force stretched out, as it were, over the body which it animates in this world, while the narrower segments in between represent the periods between lives when the soul contracts in upon itself in the purely spiritual surroundings of the other world.

The *ankh*, or ansate cross, the Egyptian symbol for immortality, is carried only by gods. Its appearance on the top of the *djed* column implies that gods like Osiris and his predecessor Atum were simply men who had attained perfection by leading just lives in former times, and it is therefore within the grasp of any man at any time, having worked his way up the column of psychogenic evolution, to attain immortality by following their example.

The arms that are stretched upwards from the *ankh*, with hands lightly touching the solar disc, signify that in its state of highest perfection human intelligence is just able to reach up and make contact with the divine Intelligence, shown in the shape of the sun god Ra.

10) It was disputed in ancient times whether Cadmus, the legendary founder of Boeotian Thebes, was an Egyptian or a Phoenician (see *Pausanias* ix. 12): the story of the Sphinx, coupled with the fact that the Greek town's name was the same as the Greek name for the Egyptian capital, suggests the existence of a connection between Thebes and Egypt at a very early date. Our suggestion is that Cadmus was a Phoenician who planted a settlement close to the site of a much older Egyptian colony, and that the 'Sparti' or 'sown men' who, according to the legend, sprang up out of the ground when he sowed the dragon's teeth were armed men from that colony who tried unsuccessfully to fight him off. In that case, the founding of the abbey would date back to pre-Cadmean times.

In Classical Greek times Thebans were a by-word for their stupidity. A very stupid Athenian boy would be referred to by his schoolmates as a 'Theban pig'. The low standard of intelligence that this implies would be the natural genetic result of the systematic draining away over several centuries of all the more intelligent Theban children to a seminary whence they did not return to their families but were dispersed to different temples all over Greece.

Another result of the Sphinx's creaming off of the city's brains was to produce in those who remained an inveterate hatred of their more intelligent neighbours in other Greek cities. Whenever two populations live side by side and there exists an appreciable difference between their respective average levels of intelligence, the duller population will conceive a hatred against the brighter for being quicker to seize opportunities for self-advancement and for having greater success in gaining the prizes of competitive endeavour. This is the root cause of anti-semitism in modern times, and of witch hunts in medieval times. In the case of the Thebans, such was their hatred of their brighter and more successful neighbours in Athens that when the whole of Greece was threatened with enslavement by the armies of the King of Persia they sent a force to fight alongside the Persians against the Athenians at Marathon. Later they helped to destroy the Athenian empire by siding with the Spartans in the Peloponnesian war.

There are signs that a similar process is at work today causing hatred and bitterness in places where Roman Catholics and Protestants live side by side in separate enclaves. In communities in which the educational system is controlled by the Roman Catholic Church and there exists in consequence a tendency for many of the brighter boys to be creamed off into the priesthood where they are not allowed to marry, the average level of intelligence is bound to go down by comparison with that of Protestant communities where no such unnatural bias is exerted against the reproduction of their more intelligent sons. Sooner or later the disparity thus created is likely to erupt in war or civil strife.

3 The Ancient Wisdom

IN 671 BC Egypt, for a long time in decline, was conquered in battle by the Assyrians. After regaining its independence, which it retained for a while with the help of foreign mercenaries, the country was conquered again 150 years later by Cambyses and became part of the Persian Empire.

One effect of these conquests was to sweep away the international barriers that separated the great rival cultures of the Euphrates and the Nile and to facilitate the peaceable exchange of ideas between their respective priests and peoples. The process of syncretism in religious beliefs thus set in motion was given a further impetus when the Persian Empire was conquered by Alexander the Great in the fourth century BC and both Babylon and Egypt were merged with Greece and Macedon in one vast domain. But Alexander's empire was also short lived. Another three centuries had to elapse before a lasting unity was achieved by which all the multifarious peoples of the ancient world from the Atlantic Ocean to the Persian Gulf were united in one peaceable society under the Caesars of Imperial Rome.

The Roman Empire can be said to have been born on the day that Cleopatra, the last of the Egyptian pharaohs, died. But the serpent that caused the death of the high priestess of Isis did not also put an end to that goddess's religion. On the contrary, it spurred on the process already begun under Cleopatra's predecessors whereby the priesthoods of Egypt spread the influence of their occult doctrines to a widening circle of adherents in Greece and Italy.

A reciprocal movement of ideas also took place from Greece and Italy into Egypt. In the first two centuries of the Christian era there appeared in Alexandria a number of books which are known as the Hermetic writings, because the principal character portrayed in them is the Osirian god Thoth, called by his Greek name Hermes Trismegistus (thrice-greatest), the messenger god of written and oral communication. Although most of the books have been lost it is known that they dealt in extended fashion both with religious beliefs and ceremonial and with science and medicine. They incorporated many concepts that were derived from Plato and other Greek philosophers, but the essence of the religious teaching set out in the most influential of them, namely the dialogue named after Asclepius (Imhotep), is a contemporary rendering of the Osirian doctrine of the judgement of the dead, coupled with an almost Buddhist view of *karma* that involves the reincarnation of human souls into other forms of life. Following Plato and Pythagoras, the author counsels the study of arithmetic, geometry, and music as the road to the understanding of the splendour of the cosmos.

One frank admission is made in the Hermetic writings, 'Our ancestors', we read, 'invented the art of creating gods'. Thoth himself was among the gods thus stated to have been purposefully created by the Egyptians. Another, more recent, god likely to have been in the author's mind was Serapis, at that time the most popular and powerful of the Egyptian pantheon, whose temple, the Serapeum in Alexandria, surpassed all others in magnificence.

Serapis was an up-dated version of Osiris, merged with the divine Imhotep, god of healing, and the bull-god Apis. He was portrayed by a huge Greek statue in the likeness of father Zeus, seated on a throne with a sceptre in his hand, a corn-measure on his head, and the three-headed dog Cerberus, guardian of Hades, at his feet. This god had been introduced into Egypt by Ptolemy Soter (323-285 BC), Alexander's hard-headed Macedonian general who inherited the Egyptian domain on the conqueror's death and founded the Ptolemaic dynasty. Planning to make the newly-founded town of Alexandria a great cosmopolitan emporium, Ptolemy recognised the need for having a powerful indigenous deity to protect the city; but he saw also that the stereotyped images of the archaic Egyptian gods would make no appeal to the foreign business community that he was desirous of attracting from the rich cities of Greece and Asia. He therefore commissioned the statue from a sculptor in Sinope, a Greek city far away on the north coast of Asia Minor, and had it brought to Alexandria where it arrived amid scenes of intense religious excitement. It was carried through the streets in a procession carefully stage-managed by the priests to inspire maximum awe at the new god's might and faith in his ability to protect the city and its people from evil. Ptolemy's story, as publicly announced, was that he had been instructed in a dream to have the statue of an unknown god brought from Sinope, and that on arrival it was pronounced by his senior advisers on religious affairs to be Osiris-Apis, or Serapis.

This story is not likely to have carried conviction amongst educated people in the sophisticated society of the Hellenistic world in the second century AD. The author of the Hermetic writings was therefore giving no secret away when he admitted that the images of the gods were man-made. What is important is that in saying this he in no way admitted that the priests who made the images were guilty of any shabby deception. He draws a clear distinction between the statues of the gods and their true natures. (The impersonations of gods by masked boys had no doubt been long since discontinued.) In that author's conception (as in that of the original King Osiris if the account given in the preceding chapter is broadly true) the gods in their physical representations were in fact, notwithstanding their human origin, meaningful portrayals of different spiritual aspects of Ultimate Reality.

(This ancient view is not without some relevance to the modern problem of religious belief, because the present-day Christian image of God the Father is historically a development of Egyptian ideas. That image springs immediately from a union of the images of pagan Father Zeus and Hebrew Jehovah. Zeus was credibly derived from Thoth (Egyptian: 'Zehuti'), while 'Jehovah' or 'Yahweh' was the name chosen by Moses to distinguish the God of Israel from the Egyptian gods, the secrets of whose religion he had doubtless learned during his upbringing at the court of Pharaoh. Likewise, the Christian image, as well as the name, of Satan, 'the adversary', with his tall ears and forked tail, is but little removed from that of Seth or Set, the enemy of Osiris.)

The Hermetic writings were among the first of many works of occult lore which purported to recapture the lost secrets of the 'ancient wisdom' of the Egyptians and Chaldaeans — already a misty legend in Greco-Roman times. The names of a multitude of sects, secret societies, and philosophic or pseudo-philosophic systems have been associated with this pursuit of the unknown from then down to the present day. They range, to name a few examples, from ancient Hermetism, Orphism, Neoplatonism, and Gnosticism, through the societies of the Manichees, Essenes, Kabbalists, Alchemists and Rosicrucians, to Theosophy, Freemasonry and the Hermetic Society of the Golden Dawn. Whereas the priesthoods of organised theistic religions teach that their respective gods are both almighty and merciful — if it were otherwise the priests' intercessions would be patently of no avail — the various doctrines of those societies and others like them tend to centre round the idea that God is neither almighty nor merciful. The central principle from which they tend to diverge in many directions is that there exists a natural order in the universe to which man and god alike are subject; that opposed to divine goodness is an opposite force of evil, the good in man residing in the spirit, the evil in the flesh; that justice is inherent in the natural order; and that the individual's destiny depends not on the arbitrary will of an all-powerful divinity but upon his own personal decisions. The doctrines of *karma* and of life after death through reincarnation are intimately connected with this philosophy because without a further incarnation in a world at least very similar to this one the injustices of this life cannot be rectified. The psyche pre-exists birth and survives death, being therefore separable from the body, with which it is often in conflict during the periods when it is conjoined with it in life on Earth. It follows that the individual's ultimate interest lies in preferring spiritual to material values and in overcoming the temptations to which he is subjected by his bodily fears and desires.

Such, in essence, is the doctrine round which the founders of the occult societies, directly or indirectly and with many variations and adaptations, may be said to have built their particular ideologies. One figure stands at the apex of the delta of those divergent streams of thought, the author and fountain head of the pure philosophy of the Cosmos: Pythagoras of Samos.

Known to his contemporaries as 'the Master of Samos', or, more simply, 'the Master', Pythagoras is the reputed inventor of the very words 'philosophy' and 'Cosmos'. He is the only man in history to have achieved world fame both as a scientist and as the founder of a new religion. This unique union of science with religion is manifestly a late echo of the age-old connection between gods and magic discussed in the previous chapter. Like all ancient priesthoods, Pythagoras divided his pupils into two classes, the initiated and the uninitiated. The latter he called *acusmatici* — a word which may be freely translated 'those who hear with their ears but do not understand'. To them he taught the principles of right living only by illustrations and parables, not by reason and logic. Nor did he disdain to follow the ancient priesthoods in their practice of the arts of magic — a practice to which new impetus had been given by a man who is believed to have been at some time his instructor, Zoroaster, founder of the Persian sect of the Magi from whom the modern word 'magic' is derived.

Many fabulous stories were current about the Master's miraculous origin and powers. It was said that his mother was a virgin and that he was begotten by the god Apollo; that he had the power to converse with birds and animals and to command storms to cease and the sea to be calm; and that he could predict earthquakes, tempests, and plagues. Most marvellous of all, one of his thighs had been seen to be of pure gold.

Deliberately contrived and skilfully cultivated by Pythagoras himself, these myths of his supernatural powers brought inestimable benefits to the society of southern Italy in which he lived. People who obstinately refuse to heed the wise counsels of philosophers, moralists and statesmen will run to obey the smallest hint from the lips of a man whom they believe to be a god. Following blindly where their divine Master led them, countless people steered their thoughts and actions in the direction in which he beckoned them towards goodness, beauty and truth, in confident expectation of receiving the reward he promised them after death of future happier lives on Earth.

Those who were fully initiated into the secrets of his cult Pythagoras named *mathematici* which may be translated 'those who learn and understand'. From the fact that the word 'mathematician' which is derived from it means what it does today the inference can be drawn that the essence of Pythagorean religious teaching was contained in the principles of arithmetic and geometry. But although the fame of Pythagoras rests more on his acknowledged pre-eminence as a mathematician than on any of his other accomplishments, and although it is known that he taught that in the last analysis 'All Things are Numbers', and 'Number is the Ultimate Reality', nevertheless no connection has been traced by modern scholars between his mathematics and his religious doctrine of reincarnation.

The ancients themselves were just as mystified. That such a connection did exist the later followers of his moral teachings did not doubt, but the secret was lost. 'When the Pythagoreans died, their secret knowledge which they had always kept locked in their hearts died with them except for some obscure points which had become talked about by outsiders but were not understood.

Pythagoras himself left no book, and those who escaped the persecutions, namely Lysis, Archippus and some others who happened to be abroad, preserved only a few vague and elusive scraps'. [1] So Porphyry, Neoplatonist philosopher of the third century AD spoke of the disaster that occurred when the Pythagorean brotherhoods which controlled the governments of many South Italian cities were massacred by popular uprisings in the first half of the fifth century BC. The Master himself was among the victims of those massacres.

Porphyry says that the secret was lost, but he did not say it was never subsequently found again. It seems that at least one man did rediscover it about a century after Pythagoras' death. Near the end of his long life the mathematician and Pythagorean philosopher Plato (c. 428-348 BC) wrote a letter to some friends in Sicily in which he declared that 'the truths that he had at heart' he had never written down because they would not have been understood except perhaps by a few who might be intelligent enough to discover them for themselves. [2] It is reasonable to infer from the context that the 'truths' that Plato was referring to were the same as the truths that Pythagoras had taught his *mathematici* about Ultimate Reality. Although, true to the tradition of all wise men of ancient times, he did not reveal the secret explicitly, it is clear that Plato incorporated the fruits of the Pythagorean teaching in allegorical fashion in his myths, and perhaps cryptically in some of the more seemingly extravagant arguments in his dialogues, notably in the *Timaeus*.

The available evidence is far from conclusive, but it is enough to warrant making the assumption, as a working hypothesis, that by some undisclosed mathematical reasoning Pythagoras first and Plato after him reached two firm conclusions: first, that Ultimate Reality consisted simply in numbers, so that in the last analysis everything consists in geometrical arrangements of numbers of points in different dimensions; and secondly that the soul is immortal and that each life on Earth is one episode in a recurrent series of lives, so ordered that any injustices suffered or inflicted in one are automatically requited by rewards and punishments in another. These two propositions go logically together because only in a purely mathematical universe is there room for enough dimensions to accommodate spiritual realities that manifestly exist inside and outside the three spatial dimensions of the material world. Only if souls return to Earth after orbiting in those higher dimensions could mathematical equations be satisfied which demand that goodness be compensated by pleasure and evil by pain.

The lesson to be drawn from the Pythagorean doctrine of reincarnation was allegorically described by Plato in the myth of Er at the end of his great dialogue *The Republic* which he devoted to the study of the nature of justice. According to the myth, Er was a man whose seemingly dead body was picked up on a battlefield and laid with others on a funeral pyre. Before the pyre was lit he came back to life and later described what he had seen 'on the other side'. The destiny of the souls of the dead, he said, was chosen by themselves according to the laws of Necessity. 'Virtue owns no master: he who honours her shall have more of her, and he who slights her, less. The responsibility lies with the chooser. Heaven is guiltless.' [3] The possible destinies of the souls ranged all the way from a heaven of marvellous beauty and joy for the virtuous to a hell where the wicked were 'flayed with scourges and dragged out by the wayside and carded like wool upon thorn-bushes.' [4]

This picture is so similar to that of the torments suffered by the souls which failed when weighed in the balance by Anubis in the Judgement hall of Osiris that it prompts the questions: did those Greek philosophers receive their doctrine from the same source as the Egyptian priests, and if so did that source deduce it from a mathematical view of the Universe?

The details of the life of Pythagoras are obscure, but it is known that as a young man he left his home in Samos, where his father was an engraver, and travelled far and wide over the continents of Europe, Africa, and Asia, acquiring knowledge wherever he went. One of his biographers, the Neoplatonist philosopher Iamblichus, listed the sources of Pythagoras' philosophy as follows: 'he learned some things from the followers of Orpheus and others from the Egyptian priests; some from the Chaldaeans and Magi; some from the mysteries performed at Eleusis, in Imbros, Samothrace, and Delos; and some also from those which are performed by the Celts, and in Iberia.' [5]

It appears from this that the young Pythagoras was initiated into the mysteries of all the religions that he studied, and it can be taken as certain that he acquired his knowledge of mathematics in Egypt and Chaldaea (Babylon).

Now it is a curious and significant fact that from about 1000 BC the further back we go in the history of civilization the more advanced do we find the state of the mathematical art. When the great astronomer and geographer Claudius Ptolemy of Alexandria (2nd century AD) decided to compile a table of trigonometrical ratios he found the Greek and Roman numeral systems currently in use quite unsuitable for that purpose because they had no logical method of expressing complex fractions of unity. Nor was the ancient Egyptian system much better because its method of calculating with fractions was clumsy and the results unclear — e.g. 0.9, or 9/10, was expressed as 1/2 + 1/4 + 1/8 + 1/40. But in the still more ancient Babylonian system which was derived from the Sumerians, the oldest known civilization in the world, Ptolemy found a numerical system admirably well designed for his purpose. This was the sexagesimal system, of which relics still survive world-wide in the division of the hour into 60 minutes of 60 seconds each and of the circle into 360 degrees.

The Sumerian sexagesimal notation as it has come down to us in cuneiform texts dug up by archaeologists was manifestly designed not, as one might expect an ancient number system to be designed, for the simple purpose of counting, but rather for calculating, and in particular for solving problems involving division. The number 60 was chosen as a base because of its large number of factors. By the use of only 14 digits (9 for units and 5 for tens, the latter being the same as the first 5 of the former, but written sideways) and, probably, a zero in medial but not terminal positions, the Sumerian mathematicians were able to multiply and divide by most numbers, and to calculate trigonometrical functions of angles, with almost the same ease as is possible today using Arabic numerals and the Hindu denary scale. [6]

The uses to which this ingenious system were put included astronomy, geodesy, and cartography. In a prefatory note to the 1805 French translation of Strabo's *Geography*, done by command of Napoleon Bonaparte, the learned classical scholar and geographer P. F. J. Gossellin (1751-1830) recorded the conclusion he had reached after a profound study of all the extant works of classical authors on geography, that far back in very ancient times an accurate measurement had been made of the length of the Earth's circumference. This conclusion was based on a comparison of the length of the stade, the linear unit used for the measurement of itineraries by Romans, Greeks, and Egyptians, with the results of the geodetic survey then recently made by French mathematicians for the establishment of units for the metric system. The latter made the metre equal to 1/10,000,000th part of the quadrant arc from the North Pole to the Equator through Paris, the total length of the Earth's polar circumference being thus precisely 40,000 kilometres. This was exactly equal to 216,000 (=60³) 'Olympic' stades of 600 Greek feet (or 500 Egyptian remens).[7] 600 Olympic stades were thus equal to exactly 1 degree of latitude, and 100 Greek feet equalled 1 second of latitude — facts of which the Greeks themselves were quite unaware.

Gossellin also examined a table of east-west distances that had been compiled by Eratosthenes (c. 284-192 BC) and copied from him by later geographers until comparatively modern times. The distances covered the known world from the Sacred Promontory (Cape St. Vincent) in Spain to Thinae (Tenasserim) on the Bay of Bengal in Thailand, and could not possibly have been measured by Eratosthenes himself. From the consistency of the errors made by the Greek geographer, Gossellin deduced that Eratosthenes had had access to a very ancient map constructed as a cylindrical projection (as is known to have been used by Phoenicians in the first century AD) and centred on the latitude of Babylon (which is about the same as that of Tyre), but that he did not understand the method of its construction. Since the Phoenicians of his day were evidently unable to inform Eratosthenes on this vital point, the French savant hazarded the guess that the original of this map might have been made in Babylonia in a former civilization, perhaps as long ago as 3600 BC and that the data on which it was based were obtained from astronomical observations.[8]

The geodetic character of the Greek foot was noticed also by E. F. Jomard, one of the savants who accompanied Napoleon to Egypt in 1798; but it was not until 1953 that attention was again called to it, this time by an English engineer, A. E. Berriman. In his important work *Historical Metrology*, Berriman surveyed the available archaeological data on all kinds of measures used by ancient civilizations in Europe and Asia, including India and China, and without any knowledge of Gossellin's work he put forward the view that the Greek stade, the Egyptian remen, and certain other linear measures were derived from sexagesimal divisions of a very ancient and accurate measurement of the Earth's circumference, and that a decimal fraction of the square on the Earth's radius was adopted as the unit for measuring land areas. He found, incidentally, that the English acre was derived from that unit; that the English inch was the measure of the side of a cube of gold that defined a unit of weight; and that a cubic English foot was used to define an ancient measure of capacity?

These last conclusions are not relevant to our immediate quest of the 'ancient wisdom', but they add their quota of weight to the evidence supporting the view put forward in later chapters regarding the Egyptian origin of the Megalithic culture of Britain. It is relevant to note in this connection that the regions that are furthest away from the centre of a civilized society's culture are the places where the standard measures used by that society are likely to be longest preserved.

Still more recently, an American professor, C. H. Hapgood, has subjected to a critical analysis a number of medieval 'portolano' maps, or navigation charts used by mariners in Europe (particularly in the Mediterranean) during the Middle Ages, and has arrived at conclusions remarkably similar to those of Gossellin without knowing anything of the latter's work or of his sources of information. [10] His broad conclusion is that the portolano maps were all derived from an original source of very great antiquity. Certain facts led him to suggest that that source might be a civilization older than any yet discovered, whose mariners had explored and mapped almost the entire globe.

A. E. Nordenskjöld had already compiled an atlas of portolano maps of the Mediterranean and pointed out that they were a great deal too accurate to have been drawn by medieval sailors. [11] Successive charts showed no signs of development, those dating from the beginning of the 14th century being just as good as those from the 16th century. It seemed as if all the maps in circulation at that time were derived from an original set that could not be improved on with the technologies then available. Moreover, the scales of distance used on all portolanos were unrelated to any units of measurement used in the Mediterranean except in Catalonia. The Catalan units were believed to have been inherited from the Carthaginians; and since Carthage was a Phoenician colony, the implication seemed to be that the originators of the portolano maps were the ancient Phoenicians whose ships sailed freely round the coasts of the western world before the advent of the Greeks and Romans.

The result of Hapgood's study was to endorse the view that the accuracy of these maps was superior to what could have been achieved in the Middle Ages. He added that it was even beyond the capacity of the technology of Ptolemy, whose new mathematical techniques had carried the art of cartography to the highest peak that it is believed to have reached before the sixteenth century. The Greeks of Alexandria were able to determine the latitudes of places with considerable accuracy, but the measurement of longitudes was still beyond them.

One of the most remarkable features of the portolano maps was that the longitudes of the places marked on them tended to be if anything even more accurate than their latitudes. A very important map dated 1513 and known as the Piri Re'is map (after the distinguished Turkish admiral to whom it belonged) shows the coasts of Europe, Africa, and America in their correct longitudes, although the means of determining longitudes that were available to European explorers at that time were still extremely crude. One of the marginal notes made by Piri Re'is on his map states that some of his source maps had come down to him from the time of Alexander the Great.

A later Turkish map of the world dated 1559, the Hadji Ahmed map, constructed on a heart-shaped projection, shows a near-perfect outline of what is now the U.S.A., on both coasts. A curious feature of the map is that the western hemisphere, whose geography might be assumed to be much less well known than that of the eastern hemisphere, is more accurately delineated than the latter. Hapgood surmised that the remarkable accuracy with which the Pacific coasts of the Americas were drawn was due to the cartographer having used the ancient source maps for this region, while for the eastern hemisphere he had abandoned these in favour of the later but less accurate maps that were based on Ptolemy's.

A similar decline in accuracy with time can be found in a comparison of two maps both made by the great Flemish geographer Mercator, author of the famous 'Mercator's projection'. One of these, dated 1538, shows the west coast of South America much more correctly than the later one of 1569 which incorporated the results of recent voyages of exploration.

The Dulcert Portolano of 1339 covers a zone of the Old World 3000 x 1000 miles in extent from Ireland in the north-west to Arabia in the south-east. The east-west distances measured on it by Hapgood, after correcting for the projection, were found to be accurate to within half a degree of longitude from one end to the other. The projection could not have been made without the use of trigonometry, nor could many of the features have been located without some method of measuring longitudes that was unknown certainly to medieval and to ancient Greek sailors, and probably also to the early Phoenicians.

On the De Canerio map, which covers Africa, the Mediterranean, and parts of Asia (1502), Hapgood found errors in east-west distances that were proportionate to the latitude — the further north the greater the errors. This suggested to him that the map had been drawn from a source map by someone who did not understand the original projection or who had a mistaken view of the radius of curvature of the Earth's surface. He found that the original projection of the De Canerio map and also that of other portolanos including the source map of the Piri Re'is projection had been an oblong construction, with degree lines of longitude at right angles to the latitudes but closer together; he surmised that the construction had involved the use of spherical trigonometry. Later copyists who did not understand the projection had imposed a square grid instead of an oblong one.

Hapgood was astonished to find exactly the same distortion in a map of China of unknown antiquity but dating certainly before the 12th century AD reproduced in Needham's *Science and Civilisation in China*. (This is essentially the same distortion as that deduced by Gosellin on the map used by Eratosthenes.) Hapgood says:

"The square grid imposed on the map is evidence of the same decline of science we have observed in the West, when an advanced cartography, based on spherical trigonometry and on effective instruments for determining latitudes and longitudes, gave way to the vastly inferior cartography of Greece — and when, later in the Middle Ages, even the geographical science known to the classical world was entirely lost . . . It seems to me that the evidence of this map points to the existence in very ancient times of a *world-wide* civilisation, the map-makers of which mapped virtually the entire globe with a uniform general level of technology, with similar methods, equal knowledge of mathematics, and probably the same sorts of instruments."

The instrument that is indispensable nowadays for determining longitudes is the chronometer, because to an observer on the Earth the heavenly bodies seem to revolve round the celestial poles once every 24 hours, and by measuring their altitudes he can calculate his distance east or west of some fixed meridian (like that of Greenwich) only if he knows what is the exact time on that meridian when he makes his observation. But it is not necessary to deduce from the accuracy of longitudes on an ancient map that the men who made it were in possession of mechanical chronometers, because there was available to them an excellent method of measuring longitudes that did not involve recourse to such an instrument. This is a method first suggested by the astronomer Hipparchus (c. 150 BC). It involves observing eclipses of the moon. At a central observatory a record is made of the altitude of a particular star at the time when an eclipse takes place. The navigator of a ship on a remote coast makes a similar record of the altitude of the same star. Months later, when the ship returns home, the records are compared, the hour angles of the star are calculated from the altitudes, and the difference, in degrees, between the two hour angles is the difference in longitude between the two places.

This method requires little technology but much careful organisation and a lot of time. Eclipses occur at irregular and infrequent intervals, so mapmaking by this method would be an extremely slow process. The method is not likely to have appealed to seafaring nations of merchant adventurers who lacked a strong central government, like the ancient Greeks and the Phoenicians. But it would be admirably suited for use by a highly organised community controlled by a mathematical élite such as we have suggested existed in the Old Kingdom of Egypt and its parent civilization on the Euphrates.

One piece of evidence found by Hapgood points to Egypt as the original source of at least one of the portolano maps. The Piri Re'is map was constructed by using plane trigonometry to fit together a number of smaller local maps, and the central reference point that was found to have been used for this purpose was a point on the Tropic of Cancer near Syene in Southern Egypt.[12]

Other evidence suggests that the oldest maps may be more ancient even than the Old Kingdom of Egypt. This evidence consists in the fact that some of the places shown on them are topographically different now from what they appear to have been at the time they were mapped. Thus, the South American component of the Piri Re'is map shows a huge river estuary for the Orinoco where now there is an extended delta; and the Hadji Ahmed map shows a broad land bridge connecting Alaska with Siberia.

These and other similar discrepancies can, of course, be explained away as due to faulty guesswork by the map-maker who was ignorant of the true conditions at those particular localities. But not so easily explained is a remarkable feature of the Oronteus Finaeus map of 1532 which shows the coastline of the whole of the Antarctic continent. Antarctica is commonly believed not to have been reached by any ship before the eighteenth century, but a land mass is nevertheless shown as covering the South Pole on many portolano maps, and its existence was certainly believed in by many people in older times, including Mercator himself. The Piri Re'is map shows it as contiguous with the South American continent, causing Cape Horn and the Drake Strait to disappear. This enlargement of Antarctica is an error common to all the maps. Its source was believed by Hapgood to be due to a mistake made long ago when a circle drawn on the original source map to represent the 80th parallel of latitude was thought to represent the Antarctic circle (66° 33'). The result was to push the coast line out so far that it overlapped South America and nearly touched South Africa.

When allowance is made for this error, the Oronteus Finaeus map shows an extraordinarily accurate map of the whole coastline. What is even more remarkable is that it shows non-glacial conditions as existing on some of the coasts and extending for some distance inland, with rivers flowing through estuaries into the sea where now there are only glaciers. The ice-free coasts include Queen Maud Land, Enderby Land, Wilkes Land, Victoria Land, and Marie Byrd Land. On the Ross Sea, opposite New Zealand, Hapgood says: 'the modern map indicates the places where great glaciers, like the Beardmore and Scott Glaciers, pour down their millions of tons of ice annually to the sea. On the Oronteus Finaeus Map fjord-like estuaries are seen, along with broad inlets and indications of rivers of a magnitude that is consistent with the sizes of the present glaciers. And some of these fjords are located remarkably close to the correct positions of the glaciers.' He describes this as 'evidence that when this source map was made there was no ice on the Ross Sea or on its coasts'.

In 1949 on one of the Byrd Antarctic Expeditions, some samples of sediments were taken from the bottom of the Ross Sea by coring tubes. Examination of these samples showed that the last warm period in the Ross Sea when fine-grained sediments were deposited by rivers ended about 4000 BC. The cores indicated that warm conditions had prevailed for a long time before that.

We thus return to the suggestion made in the last chapter (p.28) that the world's first civilization started some time before the end of the fifth millennium BC with an explosion of ideas triggered off by a mathematician who formulated the principles of trigonometry and thereby made possible the development of the arts of land survey (which includes map-making), architecture, and engineering. [13] It is only necessary to add that the science of astronomy, leading to the accurate measurement of time and the creation of a calendar, was fundamental to this civilization, and that the ability to predict the dates of eclipses would have been essential for the making of good maps in the absence of accurate chronometers.

In our story at the end of this book we assume (although the argument does not depend on the assumption) that this civilization existed, and that before it disappeared the essence of its mathematical and astronomical wisdom, including the records of eclipses that its astronomers had kept for centuries, were passed on to the mathematician-priests of its daughter civilization on the Nile. We shall see that some of the uses to which those priests put the knowledge they had thus inherited were somewhat different from those for which it was originally acquired.

Notes on Chapter 3

1) Porphyry: Vita Pythagorae 57.

2) Plato: Ep. VII 341 C.

3) Plato: Republic X 617 D: Trans. Davies & Vaughan.

4) Ibid. 616 A.

5) Iamblichus: *Vita Pythagorae* ch. XXVIII; trans. T. Taylor.

6) The Sumerian or Babylonian notation did not use a pure sexagesimal scale unit but a compound denary-sexagesimal one, with base points at 10, 60, 600, 3600, 36000 and 216000, using the factors 10 and 6 alternately. The same series was continued downwards to give fractions or subdivisions at 1/6, 1/60, 1/360, 1/3600. A detailed description of the system and how it worked is contained in a booklet by F. Thureau-Dangin, *Esquisse d'une Histoire du Système Sexagesimal* (Librairie Orientaliste Paul Geuthner, Paris, 1932).

7) The Greek foot, as measured from the dimensions of the

Parthenon and confirmed from other sources has been established as equal to 12.15 English inches (308 millimetres). On this basis, 60^3 stades of 600 Greek feet would be equal to 24852.3 miles. The Earth's polar circumference computed from the survey of Méchain and Delambre in 1798 is 24855 miles — a difference of less than 3 miles, or about 1 in 9000.

8) *Geographie de Strabon* Traduite du Grec en français à Paris, de l'Imprimerie Imperiale, 1805; Tome I; Observations Préliminaires et Génerales sur la Manière de Considérer et d'évaluer les Stades; itineraires etc., P. F. J. Gossellin.

9) A. E. Berriman, *Historical Metrology* (J. M. Dent & Sons Ltd., London, 1953).

10) Charles H. Hapgood, *Maps of the Ancient Sea-kings*. (Chilton Books, Philadelphia 1966. Revised ed.: Turnstone Books, London, 1974).

11) A. E. Nordenskjöld, *Atlas to the Early History of Cartography* (Stockholm, 1898).

12) Today the Tropic of Cancer is just over $23°27'$ north of the Equator, but it is moving very slowly south and in 2000 BC it was about half a degree further north than it is now. Its choice as a base line for mapmaking had two advantages for the ancients: (i) its location could be determined with accuracy by the fact that a vertical column casts no shadow at noon on midsummer day; and (ii) the degree of longitude there is just about 1/12th shorter than the degree of latitude — a fact which would greatly simplify calculations by people using the sexagesimal system of numeration.

13) For a detailed account of the evidence indicating that civilization began suddenly by a 'great leap forward' about that time in the Near East, see *The Birth of Civilisation in the Near East* by Henry Frankfort (Williams & Norgate, London, 1951).

(*over*) 13. The Oronteus Finaeus Map of A.D. 1532. *History has no record of the Antarctic continent having been explored before A.D. 1770*

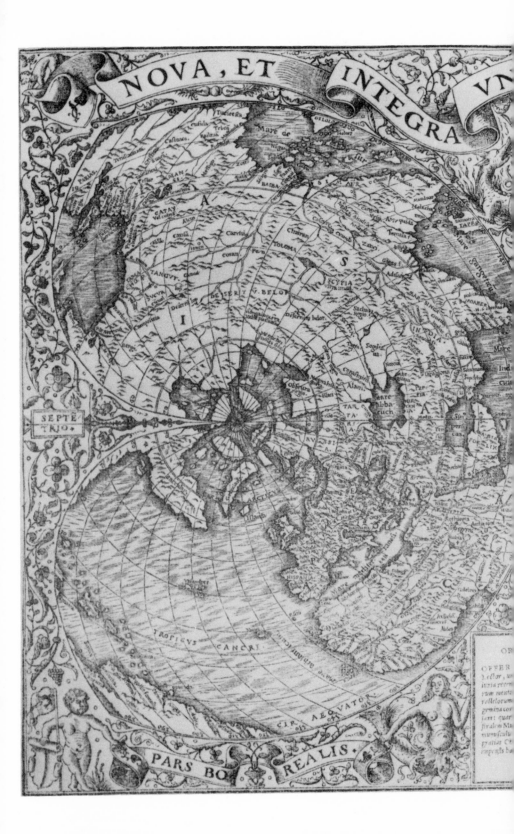

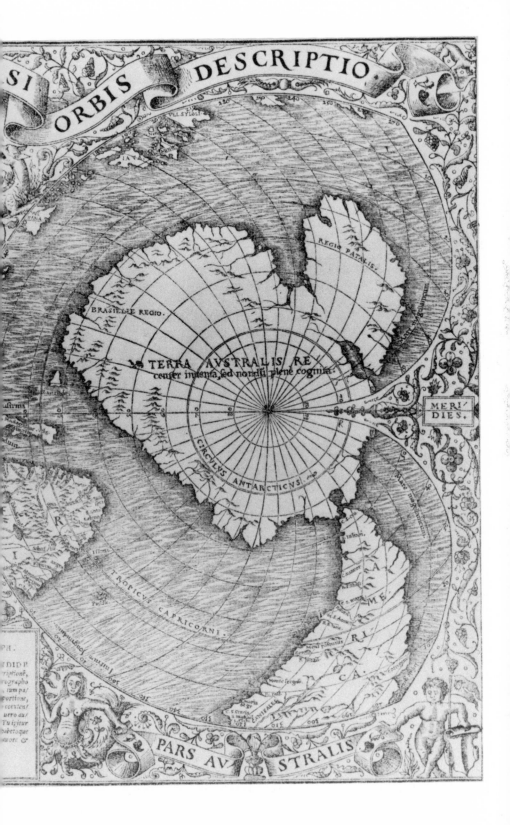

Part Two The Megaliths

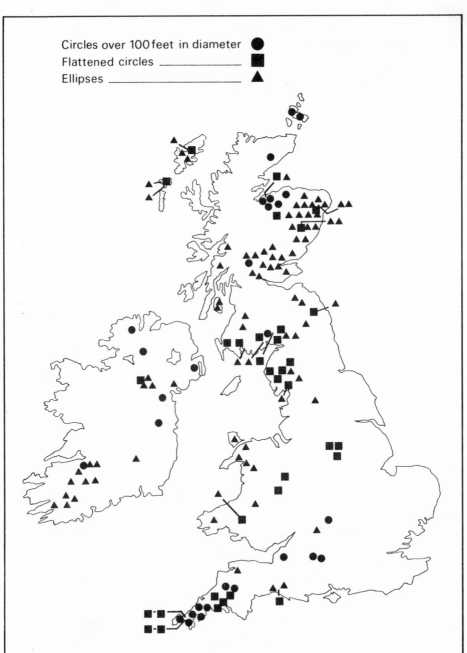

Circles over 100 feet in diameter ●
Flattened circles _____ ■
Ellipses _____ ▲

14. Map of the principal Stone Rings in the British Isles. *Egg-shaped rings, complex rings, and circular rings under 100 feet in diameter (of which there are about 600) are not shown.*

4 The Mystery of the Megaliths

MEGALITHIC STRUCTURES — that is to say, prehistoric monuments built with stones of enormous size — exist in many parts of the world. The most famous, if not the greatest number, are found in the British Isles and in Brittany in the north-west corner of France. They are of many different kinds — dolmens or cromlechs (tables of two or more uprights supporting a flat stone on top), chambered tombs, menhirs or great stones standing alone, stone rings of various sizes and shapes (circles, flattened circles, ellipses, and egg-shaped rings), and straight avenues of standing stones arranged like grids in multiple rows.

Of all the megalithic structures by far the best known and the best preserved is the circular 'temple' of Stonehenge on Salisbury Plain. We call it a temple because, in the words of the official guide, 'almost everyone agrees that Stonehenge was a temple', but we print the word in inverted commas because there is no evidence to prove that it was ever in regular use for religious worship, much less that it was originally designed for that purpose. What was the original purpose of the founders of Stonehenge is, in fact, the core of the mystery that we are here attempting to unravel.

From the point of view of sheer size and complexity of structure perhaps the most important of the megalithic sites is the great stone ring at Avebury on the Marlborough Downs about 16 miles (25 km) to the north. This is the centre of a cluster of prehistoric stones and earthworks which include the neolithic camp of Windmill Hill, the 350-foot (107 m) long West Kennet Long Barrow, and Silbury Hill, the biggest man-made mound in Europe with a height of 130 feet (40 m) and a base covering more than 5 acres (2 hectares).

Of the single megalithic stones by far the biggest is the great menhir of Er Grah (Le Grand Menhir Brisé), which lies broken in three pieces on a peninsular in Quiberon Bay, South Brittany, not far from the 1000-yard long stone avenues of Carnac. This megalith once stood over 60 feet high and was clearly visible from 10 miles across the sea. It is estimated to weigh 340 tons. This is 6 or 7 times the weight of the biggest of the huge Sarsen Stones of Stonehenge, which itself weighs 50 tons or 1½ times as much as the heaviest 'juggernaut' lorry that is allowed to travel freely on English roads today.

15. Er Grah, Le Grand Menhir Brisé. Quiberon Bay. *Weighing 340 tons, it once stood 60 feet high.*

In medieval times it was believed, not unnaturally, that the erection of the great stones at Stonehenge and elsewhere was the work of magicians. There was no other possible explanation. In his *Histories of the Kings of Britain* written in the 12th century, Geoffrey of Monmouth tells us that the stones of Stonehenge were brought to England from Ireland by the wizard Merlin to make a burial place for Britons who had been treacherously slain by the Saxon leader Hengist at a meeting to which he had invited them on Salisbury Plain. The British King Ambrosius Aurelianus (reputedly the brother of Uther Pendragon and uncle of King Arthur) wanted to build a memorial for the dead men which would last for ever, but his builders and masons could think of no way of doing this. So he sent for Merlin, the magician, who answered him thus:

' "If you want to grace the burial-place of these men with some lasting monument, send for the Giants' Ring which is on Mount Killaraus in Ireland. In that place there is a stone construction which no man of this period could ever erect, unless he combined great skill and artistry. The stones are enormous and there is no one alive strong enough to move them. If they are placed in position round this site, in the way in which they are erected over there, they will stand for ever." ' [2]

The name *Merlin* is supposed by some to be derived from that of the Celtic sky god *Myrddin*, which would link this ancient tradition of wizardry with the Druids — the priests, doctors, and wise men of the Celts who were the inhabitants of Britain and France when the Romans came. The idea is still current today that Stonehenge was a Druid temple where the Celtic priests practised their magical rites (which included human sacrifice). This theory was popularised in the seventeenth century by the antiquarian John Aubrey. Aubrey may well have been right in supposing that the Druids used Stonehenge as a temple, but that they could have built it is out of the question. Archaeology has proved that it is far too old. [3]

The first authoritative study made in modern times was done on the order of King James I, who instructed his Surveyor-General of Works, the great architect Inigo Jones, to survey Stonehenge and to report on how it came to be there. The outstanding conclusion that emerged from this professional study was that Stonehenge was a construction of such beauty and skill that it could not possibly have been build by Druids, ancient Britons or other barbarians, but must be the work of a civilized people skilled in architectural design and mathematics. The only civilized people known to Inigo Jones as having come to Britain a very long time ago were the Romans; and since the scale of the engineering works was similar to that of many Roman works that he had seen on the continent, he not unnaturally concluded that Stonehenge was built by the Romans.

It is tempting to use this report to illustrate the superiority of modern archaeological knowledge over that which existed in the time of James I. One can smugly point out how wrong the seventeenth century architect was to attribute to the Romans a work which we now know to have been constructed some 2000 years before Julius Caesar set foot in Britain.

But this would be unfair because it would ignore Jones' most important conclusion, which has never been disproved, that Stonehenge was built by civilized people. Until an architect of equal distinction comes forward to state it as his considered opinion that, judging from the architectural evidence alone, Stonehenge appears to be the work of illiterate barbarians using pre-civilized methods of design and construction — i.e., methods that did not involve the preparation of drawings, the use of pens, paper, rulers or compasses, or the making of any calculations more complex than the simple sums that could be carried out in a primitive person's head — until then, Inigo Jones' view is entitled to hold the field as the best extant professional view regarding the quality of the human minds that inspired that majestic edifice.

Unfortunately no great engineer has expressed a similarly authoritative opinion on the quality of the brains that devised practical methods by which to quarry, shape, transport by land and water, and erect stones weighing up to 50 tons. The lintels of the great trilithons had to be raised about 20 feet before being lowered onto the uprights to which they were secured by pre-cut tenon and mortice joints. The lintels of the sarsen circle were jointed to one another by tongue-and-groove joints and levelled with such accuracy that it is scarcely conceivable that this could have been done by eye alone without the use of instruments.

16. Aerial View of Stonehenge.

But the inhabitants of Britain in 2000 BC were, we are told, uncivilized neolithic farmers who lived in small village communities, did not know the use of metals, and could not read or write. In efforts to reconcile these archaeological findings with the facts of the megalithic structures a great deal of ingenuity has been displayed in devising methods by which the great stones could have been erected without the use of tools or apparatus beyond what is thought likely to have been available to such primitive people.[4] Practical experiments have shown that such methods were indeed possible. But did the scientists who carried out those experiments design them entirely in their heads and organise their execution by oral communication only without at any time putting pen to paper? Could they possibly have carried them out successfully if to do so had been made a condition of the experiments? The question that has to be asked is not whether it was physically possible for intelligent men with modern knowledge and means of communication to build a megalithic circle with Stone Age tools, but whether the minds of illiterate barbarians, blinkered by primitive superstitions and adapted only to cope with the restricted physical conditions of Stone Age life could have become so ingenious, so emancipated, so intellectually and socially mature that they were able of a sudden first, to conceive the abstract idea of building such a structure, next to make the considerable mental effort needed to plan it in detail without making any drawings and finally, to organise themselves so as to make the colossal and prolonged physical efforts that were needed to cut and move the stones and set them up on the site. Professor R. J. C. Atkinson has estimated that merely for the transport of the 81 sarsen stones from nearby Avebury to Stonehenge not less than 1500 men were needed working continuously with not more than a few days rest between trips, for 5½ years; for the building of Silbury Hill, which is now assigned a date as far back as 2750 BC, 500 men would have had to work for 15 years — an effort which, expressed in economic terms as a percentage of the gross national product of the local community, it has been estimated would be comparable with the effort made by the United States in the realisation of their space programme. For the whole of the work involved in building the first two stages of the Stonehenge structure, Professor G. S. Hawkins guessed that something like a quarter of a million man-days would have been necessary, and for the third stage perhaps a million and a quarter.

The Sphinx and the Megaliths

Figures of this order show that not only was an architectural and engineering genius needed to conceive and design these monuments, but organising ability of very high quality was necessary to carry out their construction. In fact, the work could probably not have been undertaken at all without the use of some means of communication more reliable than simple word of mouth.

17. Stonehenge. *Sunrise over the Heel Stone on Midsummer Day*

Starting from the well-known fact that, viewed from the centre of the Stonehenge circle, the sun is seen to rise exactly over the heel-stone on midsummer day, the theory was tentatively advanced some generations ago and has been argued more loudly in recent years that some of the megalithic structures were originally built as astronomical observatories. Archaeologists who studied the early evidence generally remained unconvinced by it because they regarded its implications as incompatible with their findings regarding the level of culture reached by the inhabitants of Britain in the third and second millennia BC.

A vigorous controversy between archaeologists and astronomers was sparked off by the appearance of G. S. Hawkins' book *Stonehenge Decoded* in 1966. Because of the important light that it threw on the problem the course of the argument is summarised in some detail in Chapter 8 below. The conflict ended in a stalemate, with the archaeologists claiming the victory, though neither side yielded from its position. As further studies have proceeded, however, notably those by Professor A. Thom, the trend of their results has been consistently in the direction of supporting the astronomical theory. Not one significant fact tending to refute it has emerged, despite the urge to find one that was engendered by the warmth of the controversy.

In December 1972 a multi-disciplinary conference organised by the Royal Society in conjunction with the British Academy was held in London in a seasonably cool and friendly atmosphere. The subject for general discussion was 'The Place of Astronomy in the Ancient World', but the issue that was the real focus of interest was the place of astronomy in the megalithic culture of north-west Europe in particular.

In his two books *Megalithic Sites in Britain* (1967) and *Megalithic Lunar Observatories* (1971) Professor Thom had described the results of some hundreds of surveys of megalithic sites that he had carried out over many years with meticulous accuracy over the whole area from the Orkney Islands and the Outer Hebrides to the south of Brittany. The questions to which those attending the conference wanted to know the answers were centred on those results (described more fully in Chapter 9 below). Did Professor Thom's discoveries of hundreds of astronomically significant alignments of megaliths really substantiate his claim that they proved the sites to have been laid out as lunar observatories, or were the alignments just fortuitous? Did the builders really possess a standard unit of measurement which they kept for hundreds of years and used at all their many sites and which yet never varied by as much as a millimetre from its constant value of 32.64 inches (829 mm)? Did they really set out to construct, by means of complex geometry based on Pythagorean triangles, non-circular rings such that the length of the perimeter was exactly three times the length of the largest diameter? And did they really construct in the extreme north of Scotland and in Britanny tapering grids of stones which served as computers for the solution of quadratic equations to enable them to extrapolate the complicated motions of the moon from point observations and so determine the precise dates on which eclipses would occur?

As was to be expected at a conference of this nature, no unequivocal answer was given then and there to any of these questions. But it can be asserted nevertheless that the astronomical view prevailed. The nature of the evidence is such that unless it is challenged and refuted on mathematical grounds the claims made must be accepted. The scientific method of enquiry does not allow definite quantitative evidence derived from accurate surveys of ancient works to be rejected simply on the ground that it leads to a conclusion inconsistent with a currently accepted general theory regarding the level of culture attained by the people who constructed them. Therefore, since no authoritative voice was raised to challenge the technical evidence — on the contrary, such statistical evidence as was produced by Professor D. G. Kendall and others tended to support it on the particular points that were independently investigated — the conclusion is that the 'astronomical view' must be taken from now on as the one that holds the field.

This does not solve the mystery of the megalithic culture, but rather deepens it. It makes it more than ever necessary to look for a way of reconciling the mathematical with the archaeological evidence. On the one hand we are told by archaeologists of the highest distinction that, at the time when the great stones were erected here, Britain was inhabited by uncivilized people still living in the Stone Age in a primitive state of culture. On the other hand mathematicians and astronomers of equal eminence tell us that the stones were erected by men who had a very considerable knowledge of geometry and astronomy, a knowledge sufficiently advanced, it would seem, to enable them, with a little tuition in the use of modern techniques, at least to pass the entrance examination into a modern university if not actually to get a B.Sc. degree. (Professor Thom's explanations of the fan-shaped arrangements of stones that he found in several places in Caithness, and of the mile-long tapering avenues at Carnac are beyond the comprehension of most modern readers whose mathematical education stopped below university level.) [5]

18. Carnac. *Rows of 3000 megaliths 1 Km long, deduced by Prof. Thom to have been used in conjunction with the great menhir of Er Grah as a computer for the prediction of eclipses.*

The Sphinx and the Megaliths

The main purpose of this book is to suggest a possible solution to this mystery. Our basic approach is to abandon the assumption that because the stones were erected when Britain was inhabited by primitive people it follows that they must have been erected by those people. We postulate instead that a colony of highly civilized people came to Britain from Egypt and established themselves in separate communities alongside the older barbarian communities with whom they exchanged knowledge of certain arts and customs but who otherwise remained true to their traditional ways of life.

Egypt was the only civilized country in existence within reasonable reach of Britain at the time Stonehenge was founded. Some time ago it was suggested by Professor Atkinson that the source of the megalithic people's knowledge of stone-masonry was the Bronze Age cultures of Minoan Crete and Mycenaean Greece. Traces of a number of carvings of axeheads and daggers which suggested a connection with those cultures were discovered by him on the sarsen stones at Stonehenge, and these together with certain architectural similarities led him to suggest that a powerful Wessex chieftain might have employed a Mycenaean architect to superintend the construction of that monument. But the sarsen stones formed no part of the original structure of Stonehenge. The first circle of megaliths that was erected there was built of 'bluestones' brought from South Wales at a time when the Aegean civilization was still in its infancy. The axe and dagger carvings are therefore of no help in solving the mystery of the origin of Stonehenge, but they could be a valuable clue to its middle history.

There is nothing new in the idea that the megalithic people came from Egypt. That country has often been cited as a possible source of ancient cultures that came into being not only in north-west Europe but in places much further away, including Central and South America.[7] What follows is simply a new version of an old idea. As such, our theory is open to all the objections that have been raised against similar theories in the past.

Not the least of these objections is one of which much has been made in recent years by archaeologists who cite the immense age of the oldest megalithic sites and the absence of any similar structures of greater age elsewhere as evidence of their being the products of an indigenous neolithic culture that grew up in north-west Europe independently of the growth of civilization in

Egypt and the Aegean. Dates as long ago as 4000 BC are now assigned to the oldest megalithic tombs in Brittany — several centuries before the First Dynasty in Egypt and over 1000 years before the building of the pyramids.

Here it is necessary to distinguish between different components of what is loosely termed the 'megalithic culture'. That term is used to describe not a single homogeneous entity as might be supposed, but a whole complex of cultures and sub-cultures that were established by people of several different racial origins and which spread over a large area of Europe, Africa and Asia over a long period of time. The origins and inter-relations of the several elements are the subject of keen debate among archaeologists. Our concern here is exclusively with the stone circles and avenues which were built in the third and second millennia BC and are peculiar to Britain and Brittany. Regarding the older structures we have only one suggestion to offer.

In his book *The Key*, J. P. Cohane, an amateur etymologist, recorded the conclusions he reached at the end of a detailed study of place-names from all over the globe, supported by evidence of some ancient customs and of the names of certain animals, plants, and parts of the body. His first conclusion was that the evidence he had collected indicated 'a strong likelihood that in ancient times, before the Phoenicians, the Carthaginians, the Egyptians, the Greeks, and the Romans, certain key names and words were taken out in all directions from the Mediterranean, in some instances by water routes, and that these same names and words can still be found, in spite of corruptions, in the names of rivers, mountains, volcanoes, and waterfalls, lakes, islands, regions, towns and cities, scattered all across the face of the earth.' Further study brought him to his second conclusion, that the key names could be broken down into two groups on a geographical basis. 'The names in the first group, which appears to be older, are to be found in *all* parts of the world. Those in the second group are to be found on a more intensified level but in a *limited* portion of the world. This latter set of names permeates the Mediterranean basin, Europe, Africa, and parts of Asia, moves across the Atlantic into the West Indies, into Brazil, and are found along the gulf coast of Central America and up the East coast of North America. They are not, however, to be found in any significant degree on the continent of North America, in Central America, Mexico, Peru, or Chile. They are also strikingly absent from China and in the Pacific, from and including the Hawaiian Islands.'[8] To both groups of names Mr. Cohane ascribes a Semitic origin, largely, it seems, because they appear in ancient Semitic legends including the Book of Genesis.

These are one man's subjective conclusions not based on any scientific analysis; but for what they are worth they tend to support the idea adumbrated here in the two preceding chapters: that the first (pre-Sumerian) civilization was founded in the fifth millennium BC in the valley of the Euphrates, whence groups of men set sail to explore and map the entire globe using the mathematical and metrological tools that had been given them by their founder. We suggest that one group of explorers stayed in Britain or France, whether by choice or through necessity, and founded the first megalithic culture. These were the people who built the early Passage Graves. Coming to the rocky coasts of western Europe from the vast alluvial plain of lower Mesopotamia where rocks are unknown, they reacted like a child presented with his first box of building bricks. They took a boyish delight in discovering all the wonderful things that could be done with this exciting new material, stone. But they were few in number, and in the course of centuries without contact with other civilized communities they mixed with the indigenous Stone Age inhabitants and their civilization reverted to barbarism.

Meanwhile the seeds of civilization had taken root in the Nile valley and there produced the flower of the Old Kingdom culture. This was the source from which the second group of explorers came to found the great megalithic culture of the third and second millennia BC. These are the people that we are concerned with here.

In trying to discover the secrets of their mysterious activities we shall follow many clues gleaned not only from the main fields of study directly involved, namely archaeology and astronomy, but from such other fields as classical history and literature, mythology, occultism and numerology, and, most important of all, the sadly neglected field of historical metrology.

In the following chapters we first discuss the clues that strike us as significant before putting forward in the form of a connected narrative our theory as to how they should be interpreted and how the whole mass of miscellaneous facts might be ordered to make a sensible and coherent story. The reader of detective fiction who is in the habit of reading the last chapter first so that he can interpret the clues as he goes along in the light of the detective's final reconstruction of the crime may like to turn now to chapters 11 to 13 and read there the author's suggested reconstruction of this phase of British prehistory before turning to the intervening chapters to see what evidence is adduced to support it.

Notes on Chapter 4

1) R. J. C. Atkinson, *What is Stonehenge: A Guide for Young People* (HMSO, London,1964).

2) Geoffrey of Monmouth, *The History of the Kings of Britain* viii 10. Trans. Lewis Thorpe (Penguin Books, London,1966).

3) For a fuller account of the many ancient legends associated with Stonehenge the reader is referred to the first chapter of G. S. Hawkins' book *Stonehenge Decoded* (Souvenir Press, London,1965).

4). See R. J. C. Atkinson's article 'Neolithic Engineering', *Antiquity* Vol. XXXV p.292 (1961).

5) A. Thom, *Megalithic Lunar Observatories* (Clarendon Press, Oxford 1971, pp. 83-105); *Journal for the History of Astronomy* iii, 11-26 (1972).

6) R. J. C. Atkinson *Stonehenge* (Hamish Hamilton, London,1956, p.164).

7) A concise summary of the evidence indicating that the pre-Columbian civilizations of the Incas, Aztecs, Toltecs, and Mayas of Peru, Mexico, and Guatemala were derived from Egypt is contained in an essay entitled *Isolationist or Diffusionist* by Thor Heyerdahl in *The Quest for America* (ed. Geoffrey Ashe, Pall Mall Press, 1971). To an ordinary layman the case there presented by the author of *Kon-Tiki* and *The Ra Expeditions* appears incontrovertible. The arguments based on identical or very similar customs, skills, and art forms are strong enough to carry conviction by themselves; when supported as they are by botanists who have shown that certain plants useful to man and not indigenous on the American continent must have been introduced there from the Old World in pre-Columbian times there is surely no longer any reasonable room for doubt. A convincing case is also made by Betty Meggers in her essay *Contacts from Asia* in the same volume for believing that the Valdivia and Bahia cultures of Ecuador were strongly influenced by immigrants from Japan. The first of these cultures dates back to around 3000 BC. Heyerdahl's own adventurous expeditions have effectively demolished the main argument against the 'diffusionist' view of the origin of the American

civilizations by proving that boats of a kind known to have been used by the ancient Egyptians could indeed cross the Atlantic with favourable currents along the 'Columbus route' from North Africa to the Gulf of Mexico.

8) J. P. Cohane, *The Key* (Turnstone Books, London,1973, pp. 18 & 21).

5 The Archaeology of Stonehenge

THE EVIDENCE available to the archaeologists at Stonehenge is bafflingly meagre, but with it they have performed miracles of detection that have resulted in the emergence of a fairly clear picture of the various stages of construction and destruction through which the monument has passed in the course of its long history. For a detailed and authoritative account the reader is referred to Professor Atkinson's book *Stonehenge*. Here it is possible to do no more than summarise the main conclusions that have a bearing on our story. (See plan on page 147.)

Three main stages of construction have been distinguished. In the first, Stonehenge I, the builders dug the circular ditch that surrounds the 'temple', and from the material so excavated they made the bank that now stands little more than 2 feet above ground level on the inside of the ditch but which was originally at least 6 feet high and about 20 feet wide. The bank was built in a true circle of about 320 feet (98 metres) diameter.

Just inside the bank they dug a series of 56 flat-bottomed holes evenly spaced round the circumference of a circle about 280 ft (85 m) in diameter concentric with the bank. These are the 'Aubrey holes', named after John Aubrey who discovered them by noticing cavities in the turf that covered them. What purpose was intended to be served by the Aubrey holes, and why there were 56 of them, are two of the most puzzling questions to which we have to suggest answers. One archaeological clue consists in the cremated remains of human bodies which were found in some of the holes. The ashes were apparently buried there soon after the holes were dug, and were found mixed in with the chalk rubble that had been dug from the holes and then shovelled back in, some of it having been burnt meanwhile. Remains of other cremations have been found buried under the turf in the ditch and on the bank.

Some 80 feet outside the ditch on the north-east side of the circle the builders erected the famous Heel Stone, a huge

19. (over) Stonehenge

undressed block of 'sarsen' stone, a kind of natural sandstone of which outcrops are found on the Marlborough Downs about 20 miles away. It stands leaning inwards, 16 feet tall, and its bluntly pointed tip viewed from the centre of the circle marks with tolerable accuracy the point on the horizon where the sun rises on midsummer day. According to an old legend, the stone was thrown by the Devil at a certain friar whom it struck on the heel, the imprint of the blow being supposedly visible on the outer face of the stone. Atkinson thought it likely that the story was invented to explain the stone's name, for which no other derivation is known.

It is possible that the four Station Stones were also erected in the Stonehenge I period, although they have also been assigned to Stonehenge III. Only two of these stones now exist. The two which have disappeared were erected on mounds which still remain. Like the Heel Stone, the Station Stones are undressed blocks of 'sarsen' stone. They form a rectangle with its corners on the circumference of the Aubrey hole circle, some of the holes being covered by the mounds. They provide important evidence for the astronomical theory, as we shall see.

One other feature of Stonehenge I also has important astronomical significance. This is a series of holes dug apparently to hold wooden posts just outside the bank on what later became the Avenue or entrance causeway. They are arranged in a kind of irregular grid pattern west of the main axis of Stonehenge that runs north-east/south-west from the Heel Stone through the centre of the circle. Just inside them, in the gap in the bank through which the Avenue passes, are two big stone holes which are believed to date from the same period.

In Stonehenge II the Avenue was made and the bluestones were triumphantly conveyed along it at the end of their arduous journey from Pembrokeshire across the Bristol Channel and up the Bristol Avon, to be erected in a double ring in the 'Q' and 'R' holes close to the present bluestone circle. The exact locality in the Prescelly mountains in north Pembrokeshire from which the bluestones were brought was established in 1923 beyond any possibility of doubt by Dr. H. H. Thomas of the Geological Survey, who showed that only there do the three varieties of dolerite, rhyolite and petrified volcano ash of which they are composed occur together in a natural state. It is an area of about one square mile at the extreme eastern end of the range, between the summits of Carn Meini and Foel Trigarn.

Why the bluestones were brought on that long and perilous journey when equally good material was to be had near at hand is another mystery. It has been suggested that the Prescelly mountains were regarded as specially sacred for some religious reason and that therefore stones brought from there would be imbued with magic properties for the healing of ailments. Support for such a view appears to be given by Geoffrey of Monmouth in the continuation of the passage quoted in the last chapter:

> 'These stones' (said Merlin) 'are connected with certain religious rites and they have various properties which are medicinally important. Many years ago the Giants transported them from the remotest confines of Africa and set them up in Ireland at a time when they inhabited that country. Their plan was that, whenever they felt ill, baths should be prepared at the foot of the stones; for they used to pour water over them and to run this water into baths in which their sick were cured. What is more, they mixed the water with herbal concoctions and so healed their wounds. There is not a single stone among them which hasn't some medicinal virtue.'

Professor Atkinson commented as follows on this passage:

> 'For a long time the story of the transport of the stones of Stonehenge from Ireland was regarded as a mere flight of fancy. But the growing belief that the bluestones came from some locality a long way off, finally identified as Pembrokeshire in 1923, and the high probability that they were carried from there most of the way by water, puts an entirely different complexion on the story. The correspondence between the legend and the fact is so striking that it cannot be dismissed as mere coincidence; for to do so imposes at least as great a strain upon credulity as to suppose that behind this correspondence there lies a genuine memory of recorded events. Professor Stuart Piggott, who has discussed in detail the sources used by Geoffrey of Monmouth, concludes that we cannot rule out the possibility that he had access to written or oral tradition, now lost but then still current in Wales, which embodied the story of the carrying of the bluestones from Prescelly to Stonehenge. Among the many extraordinary hypotheses concerning Stonehenge this is by no means the least

credible. For the story of the carriage of so many stones over so great a distance would be one worthy of note and remembrance even in the Middle Ages, and still more so among the illiterate societies of prehistoric times in which the oral transmission of tales of legendary and heroic feats was commonplace.' [1]

This is all very true; but an illiterate society is not nearly such a good preserver of records as a literate one, especially if the illiterate is not a homogeneous society but consists of successive incursions of barbarians of several quite different cultures. These in fact, are just the conditions in which one would most expect all memory of the exploits of the earlier cultures to be lost. If Geoffrey of Monmouth's history does in fact contain scraps of information relating to events that occurred three thousand years before he lived, that could only be because memories of those events had been handed down from generation to generation uninterruptedly throughout that time. Experience of the most recent Dark Ages through which European history has passed suggests that the ideal repository for the safe keeping of ancient memories in troubled times is a holy order of priests holding fast to their faith in an inviolable sanctuary for century after century while civilizations rise and fall in the world outside.

The statement that Geoffrey puts into the mouth of the magician Merlin, that the stones were set up by giants who came 'from the remotest confines of Africa' lines up with our suggestion that the founders of Stonehenge were Egyptians. And the connection with magic, in regard both to the healing properties of the stones themselves and to the means by which they were set up, is redolent of the sphinx-like priest-scientists of Ra-Harakhte.

In Stonehenge III the double circle of bluestones was dismantled and the stones were erected in the present single circle and horseshoe; the gigantic sarsen stones were brought from Marlborough Down and set up in the circle where they now stand and in the great central horseshoe of trilithons.

These operations established the final ground plan of the temple, which was never subsequently changed. A priest entering from the outside would have passed first through a ring of newly shaped and dressed sarsen uprights surmounted by lintels forming a continuous level surface all round; then through a rather ragged ring of worn down bluestone uprights; and lastly into the great horseshoe of five sarsen trilithons within which were the remains of a smaller horseshoe of bluestone uprights.

The sarsen horseshoe was symmetrically arranged with the biggest trilithon in the centre astride the main axis, facing the rising midsummer sun, and the two smallest at the outer ends. In front of the central trilithon is the Altar Stone, so called because it lies horizontally across the line of the main axis in a position where one might expect an altar to have been built. No one knows whether it ever stood upright, or if so where. Sixteen feet long by 3 ft. 4 in. wide by 1 ft. 9 in. thick (5 x 1 x ½ metres) it was broken in two by the fall of the great trilithon, of which one upright lies across its centre and the lintel across one end. This is consistent with the theory that it once formed the top of a table, supported by two smaller stones which were removed long ago.

The most significant feature of the Altar Stone is its composition. It came from Pembrokeshire like the bluestones, but it is composed of pale green micaceous sandstone and its place of origin is not the Prescelly mountains but the Cosheston Beds on the shores of Milford Haven. This strikes a blow at the theory that stones from the Prescelly mountains were chosen because of the specially sacred nature of the site. The stone that was placed nearest the centre of the Holy of Holies came not from a mountain at all but from a valley by the seashore.

At a late stage in Stonehenge III two rings of holes known as the 'Y' and 'Z' holes were dug outside the Sarsen circle but inside the Aubrey holes, apparently in order to receive other large stones; but there is no trace of any stones having been erected in them and the conclusion has been drawn that they were abandoned on a change of plan. The diameter of the outer ring of 'Y' holes is about 170 feet (52 m), and that of the inner 'Z' holes, something less than 130 feet — say 40 metres.

The dates that were ascribed by Professor Atkinson in 1956 for the three main stages of construction are as follows:-

Stonehenge I ...... 1900 - 1700 BC
Stonehenge II ...... 1700 - 1600 BC
Stonehenge III ...... 1500 - 1400 BC

These were described as being 'very approximate' dates. Evidence obtained more recently from the radiocarbon dating of an antler pick found in the primary silt of the outer ditch, 3 inches from the bottom, put the date of Stonehenge I back to 2180 BC ± 105. Another radiocarbon dating indicated that the transition from Stonehenge II to Stonehenge III took place in the 17th century BC, and that the digging of the 'Y' and 'Z' holes was done much later in the 13th century BC.

A further impulse in the direction of the earlier dating of megalithic monuments was given by excavations on Silbury Hill. When he began digging there in 1967 Professor Atkinson expected that the date of its construction would be found to be in the Early Bronze Age, about 1600 BC. But radiocarbon tests of exceptionally well preserved fragments of vegetable matter taken from the centre of the hill revealed a date of 2145 BC ± 95 years.

Still more recently the whole system of radiocarbon dating has had to be revised as a result of research carried out in California on some very ancient trees called bristlecone pines. The conclusion has been drawn that all radiocarbon dates obtained from Bronze Age and Stone Age objects have been underestimated by several centuries. The central dates now assigned for the construction of Stonehenge I and Silbury Hill are 2775 and 2745 BC respectively. This makes them roughly contemporary with, if not slightly earlier than, the early pyramid-builders in Egypt. But past experience enjoins caution in the acceptance of new scientific dating techniques as final, lest some new (and always unexpected) discovery throws the whole system back into the melting-pot.

Notes on Chapter 5

1) R. J. C. Atkinson, *Stonehenge* (Hamish Hamilton, London 1956; pp. 184-5). It might be added that the names *Killaraus* (p. 63) and *Pres-celly* are not so dissimilar that they could not have a common derivation. There is no place called Killaraus in Ireland.

6 Inferences
from Archaeology

QUITE APART from the doubts that have been cast by astronomers on the conventional 'neolithic farmer' theory of the megalithic culture, there are several purely achaeological reasons for considering that theory to be less probable than one that pictures the founders of the culture as well educated men who came to Britain from a civilized country.

Sixty years ago, in 1913, the Australian anthropologist Sir Grafton Elliot Smith wrote a paper in which he ascribed the origin of the megalithic people's chambered tombs to the *mastabas* built in Egypt in the early part of the third millennium BC. Referring to this paper in his book on prehistoric Wales, Sir Mortimer Wheeler said 'the general analogy between the *mastabas* and many types of chambered tomb is too close to be altogether accidental'.[1]

If the similarity was not accidental, it could only have come about as a result of a movement of people from Egypt to England about that time. That was the epoch of the great Third and Fourth Dynasties when the civilization of the Old Kingdom of Egypt was at its height. There was no other developed civilization of any kind within reasonable reach of the British Isles, nor was there any other culture in the world that had yet learned the arts of quarrying and transporting by land and water huge blocks of stone, cutting and tooling them to shape, and erecting them one on top of another.

The stones of the Egyptian pyramids were cut in rectangular blocks and laid with meticulous accuracy in horizontal layers. The step principle invented by Imhotep and applied by him in the Step Pyramid of Zoser at Saqqara was modified and perfected in the centuries that followed, but it was never abandoned. The steps were made smaller and the ends were revetted with blocks so shaped that they fitted together to make a perfectly smooth exterior sloping surface; but if these facing stones are removed, as they were many years ago from the Great Pyramid of Cheops to build mosques in Cairo, the steps stand out, making a natural stairway to the top.

20. Silbury Hill

Excavations under the direction of Professor R. J. C. Atkinson in the last few years have revealed many details previously unknown about the methods used in the construction of Silbury Hill. That pyramid was not built in the way one might expect Stone Age aboriginals to have built it, by simply digging a ditch and shovelling the material from it into a heap in the middle, as children build sand-castles on the beach. Far from it. Silbury Hill was a complex piece of engineering involving advanced methods of construction similar to those used in the Egyptian pyramids. For the main part of the hill the material dug from the ditch was laid systematically in horizontal layers, the outer edges of which were revetted by means of sloping retaining walls made of large blocks of chalk. The method was applied with such accuracy that the centre point of the topmost layer is within 2½ feet of a vertical line drawn through the centre of the base. [2]

Here, then, at Silbury Hill is another similarity between ancient British and Egyptian architecture that is surely 'too close to be altogether accidental'.

Perhaps the similarity extends, too, to the purposes which the respective pyramids were built to serve. The Egyptian pyramids were mausoleums of a rather special character, in that they were built during the life-time of the Pharaoh to house his body when he was dead. The burial chamber was hewn out of the rock on which the pyramid was built, and the approach to it for the funeral procession was by means of a sloping passage leading down from a point near the edge of the base. The actual point of entry was either low down in one of the faces of the pyramid or in the ground just outside.

The construction of Silbury Hill as revealed by archaeology would seem to be consistent with the theory that the body of a man, presumably the founder of the colony, [3] was buried in the chalk underneath a small pyramid or mound built during his lifetime, the entrance to the tomb being by means of a sloping corridor starting from outside the base; and immediately after his funeral the main part of the hill was built on top, its base spreading out so as to block up and hide the entrance to the burial chamber. If that is what happened, then the body is still there (encased, if we are lucky, after the Egyptian manner in a stone sarcophagus), waiting to be discovered.

This is, of course, pure speculation. What is certain is that when archaeologists have dug into the hill at various times, expecting to find the body of some tribal chieftain buried in it *above* ground level, they have found nothing.

Let us now consider how the 'Egyptian colony' theory fits in with other archaeological features of Stonehenge.

Unlike other cultures that have emerged from primitive origins and whose gradual development can be traced through various stages as they advance from simpler to more sophisticated techniques, the megalithic culture of Britain appeared Athene-like fully developed from the start without any trace of having passed through a normal evolutionary process.

In 1954, stone No.36 (one of the two bluestone trilithon

lintels) was lifted up to enable it to be more closely examined. Professor Atkinson says:

'The exhumation of this stone allowed for the first time a full appreciation of the manual skill, no less than the feeling for form and design, possessed by those who dressed the bluestones to shape. Its basic form is that of a prism, just over 6 ft. long, whose sides taper upwards from a flat base, in which the two mortices have been hollowed out slightly askew. But it is not a true prism, for all the edges are slightly curved, and all the surfaces except the base gently rounded, so that the outlines are softened, and the stone takes on a cushioned quality which belies the unyielding hardness of its material.

The two mortices are slightly oval in plan, with interior surfaces ground smooth and almost polished. Around the inner one (to the left in Plate 21), and extending from it towards the end of the stone, is a shallow kidney-shaped depression, evidently a carefully worked seating for the top of the upright which here supported it.' [4]

21. Stone No. 36.

Stone 36 is the chief piece of evidence for the former existence of a structure of tooled bluestones which must have included at least two trilithons. The other bluestones that formed the circle were undressed. So also were the sarsen stones that formed the great circles of Avebury. These and other megaliths found at sites elsewhere in Britain, including many that date from periods considerably later than Stonehenge II, are all natural blocks of stone hauled from neighbouring hills and set up as they were with no attempt to cut them to particular shapes. Only the great sarsens of Stonehenge III are exceptions — but very significant exceptions — to this rule. But even the sarsens of Stonehenge III show no sign of technical advance over Stonehenge II. 'The standard of craftsmanship', writes Atkinson, 'is, if anything, even higher in the dressed bluestones than in the sarsens.'[5]

The evidence suggests, then, that the megalithic people, so far from having improved and developed their architectural techniques as time went on, allowed them rather to decline except for the short and very localised renaissance that produced the magnificent architecture of Stonehenge III.

According to Sir Flinders Petrie, Egyptian masons of the Old Kingdom used copper or bronze saws set with jewelled teeth, and such was the men's skill in using them that they were able to cut huge blocks of granite to an accuracy of 1/50th of an inch (0.5 mm). They also had jewelled tubular drills.[6] If such tools were in fact brought to England and used here for the first megalithic temple, it is easy to see how the standard of workmanship in later buildings would have declined. Not only would there be no social pressures in this small colony such as would have existed in the metropolitan culture to keep the human skills at their highest peak of efficiency, but the tools that the colonists brought with them would eventually have worn out and could only be replaced so long as regular contact was maintained with Egypt. If the colony came out under the auspices of the priesthood of Ra-Harakhte, that contact would in all probability have ceased when the tide of revolution swept away the hierarchy of the Old Kingdom around 2100 BC.

The author of the current official guide to Stonehenge, Mr. R. S. Newall, has suggested that the original bluestone temple may have been first erected in Wales and thence moved 'ready-made, as it were', to its present site.[7] If a vast amount of effort had been spent in cutting and tooling the stones of the trilithons to shape and carrying them and the other bluestones down from the mountains to a place nearer the sea, and if the builders had then found that the site they had chosen was, for some reason, unsuitable for its purpose, that would explain why they decided to transport the finished building, stone by stone to its new site in England rather than start afresh using local material.

It might also explain another curious feature of Stonehenge. This concerns the strange horseshoe shape of the inner sanctum or Holy of Holies of both bluestone and sarsen temples.

The invariable custom of temple architects in almost all places and at all times has been to build an open outer precinct for ceremonies attended by the general congregation and a closed inner sanctum for the priests where they could perform their specially sacred rites behind shut doors. The more inward the place, the greater its secrecy — that is the almost universal rule of religious architecture. In ancient times no uninitiated person would ever be admitted to the inmost sanctum of all or allowed to witness the mysteries that took place there. Why then do we find at Stonehenge that the outer circles of stones are closed but the inner sanctum is a horseshoe open at one end?

Not only is the horseshoe shape contrary to the principle of 'inner secrecy', but it also offends against the principle of two-way symmetry that is observed in the outer rings. If that principle had been observed in the sanctum there would have been not *five* but *six* trilithons dividing the circle in the way in which circles are geometrically best divided — into six parts. The architect would have made one trilithon — the one behind the high altar — bigger than the others, with the one facing it the next biggest, and the ones flanking them on either side smaller, and matching them in proportion. At Stonehenge one of the two big trilithons, probably the biggest, is missing from the sanctuary.

Can we perhaps discern a connection between that missing trilithon and the Altar Stone from Milford Haven? The Altar Stone is 16 feet long. The two biggest uprights of the bluestone horseshoe (stones 67 and 68) are about 13 feet. They stood at the south-western end, facing the midsummer sunrise in the north-east. Now, R. S. Newall has suggested that the principal direction towards which the monument was oriented was not north-east towards the point of mid-summer sunrise but south-west towards the point of midwinter sunset which is exactly opposite. He cites the example of the chambered tomb of Bryn Celli Ddu in Anglesey, and adds: 'The importance of this winter solstice sunset at Stonehenge was further emphasized by the Hon. John Abercromby in his book on Bronze Age Pottery (1912) where he called attention to the fact that in no religion does one enter by the door of a temple, walk some way in and then turn round to face the focus of one's worship.'[8]

R. S. Newall's suggestion is not entirely convincing. The position of the Heel Stone is powerful evidence in favour of the more usual interpretation, namely that the important date in the Stonehenge calendar was the summer solstice, and the north-east was the principal direction. If that is accepted, then, on Abercromby's argument, the biggest of the trilithons should have been the one facing south-west, i.e. the one which, so far as we know, was never erected. The uprights of that bluestone trilithon might well have been 16 feet long, to stand about 12 feet above the ground.

The transport of heavy stones by sea is a hazardous undertaking and it would not be surprising if some accidents had happened *en route*. In fact, it would be very surprising if the vast operation of carrying over 60 megaliths some 200 miles by land and water, had been carried out without a hitch. And if any stones were lost at sea, the ones most likely to go would be the biggest.

Suppose the first of the two uprights of the biggest trilithon were lost at sea, what would the organisers of the operation have done? Most likely they would have arranged for a replacement stone to be procured, not from the mountains where the originals came from but from some point close to the sea. A suitable quarry was found on the shore of Milford Haven. But if, a little later, the second of the big uprights was also sunk, then the builders might decide that their god was against them, give up the attempt, and leave open the space in the new temple where the principal trilithon should have been. The Milford Haven stone which had successfully survived the journey would then have to be used to serve some other purpose.

The loss of the main trilithon would result in the bluestone temple of Stonehenge II having its inner sanctuary built round five sixths of a circle with its open side towards the rising sun. This arrangement had certain ceremonial advantages. When Stonehenge III came to be built, the arrangement, now hallowed by time, was preserved and the five giant sarsen trilithons were erected in their present horseshoe pattern on the same alignment.[9]

The continuity of the architectural plan, the main principles of which were preserved intact throughout the long history of the building, is indeed one of the most remarkable features of the Stonehenge temple. It matches the continuity of tradition which, thanks to Geoffrey of Monmouth, seems to have reached down to modern times right from its very foundation despite changes in the culture of surrounding communities caused by successive incursions of barbarians from abroad. No changes of basic thought-patterns can be traced in the transitions between Stonehenges I, II and III. The whole monument is a cultural unity. The structure gives the appearance of having been built, altered, and rebuilt over a period of many centuries in pursuance of a single continuous purposeful objective. The men who quarried, shaped, transported, and erected the sarsen stones were evidently men inspired by the same vision using much the same techniques as those who had shaped and transported the bluestones before them and erected them in the same circular patterns. Not only the stones themselves but, as we shall see later, the astronomical alignments of Stonehenge I were carefully preserved when the structure was rebuilt in Stonehenge III.

But though there was no ideological change, there does seem to have been a sudden change in the economic circumstances of the Stonehenge community in the middle of the second millennium BC. They were able to transform the old bluestone structure, which must by then have been showing signs of dilapidation, into a new edifice that was substantially bigger and more magnificent than the original. The axe and dagger carvings that Professor Atkinson discovered on some of the sarsen stones may perhaps provide a clue to this change of circumstances, especially when considered in the light of information obtained from classical Greek authors about the later history of the temple.

If Stonehenge was founded by priests of the Egyptian sun god Ra, then it seems that at some point during the second millennium BC this northern Ra was translated into a northern version of the Greek sun god Apollo. Knowing what we do about the character of ancient priesthoods generally, and having regard to the way in which Egyptian influence in Europe, such as it was, was eclipsed by the rise of Cretan and Mycenaean power during that period, this development is exactly what might have been expected. Thanks to its famous oracle at Delphi, the church of Apollo with its headquarters on the island of Delos was now possibly the richest priesthood in the world.

We believe it was also the most advanced in the development of the arts of magic.

Notes on Chapter 6

1) R. E. M. Wheeler, *Prehistoric and Roman Wales* (Oxford University Press, London 1925). It should be added that Elliot Smith's theories are currently out of fashion in archaeological circles. He is known as a 'hyperdiffusionist', that is to say a person who held in an extreme degree the view that civilization originated in one place only and was diffused outwards from there. But the fact that Elliot Smith has been shown to be wrong in his general view that all civilizations stemmed originally from Egypt does not invalidate his observations regarding particular influences exerted by Egyptian ideas on specific European cultures.

2) It might also be observed that both Silbury Hill and the Great Pyramid have flat tops. For a detailed description of a theory put forward by B. Cotsworth at the beginning of this century that both pyramids supported a tall pole or obelisk on top and were used for the accurate measurement of the seasons of the year, see Peter Tompkins *Secrets of the Great Pyramid* (Weidenfeld & Nicolson, London 1972; pp. 121 ff). That the Great Pyramid was designed to be used for calendrical purposes may be inferred from the curious but little known fact that its base lines are not quite straight. Each of them has a very slight kink in the middle, in consequence of which the sloping faces are not plane but indented. The indentation is so slight as to be imperceptible in normal light, but for a brief moment twice a year, at sunrise on the days of the spring and autumn equinoxes, the western halves of the north and south faces are sunlit while the eastern halves are in shadow. This enables the length of the year to be determined with precision. That the ancient Britons also had some means of determining the precise length of the solar year is apparent from Diodorus' account of how they celebrated the return of the Metonic cycle every nineteenth year (chapter 7, note 4).

3) The radiocarbon dating which put the building of Silbury Hill about 30 years (within a wide margin of possible error) after the digging of the ditch at Stonehenge is consistent with the theory that the founder of Stonehenge was buried at Silbury.

4) R. J. C. Atkinson, *Stonehenge* (Hamish Hamilton, London,1956, p. 40).

5) Ibid. p. 90.

6) W. M. F. Petrie, *Ancient Egyptians (Descriptive Sociology)*, p. 58.

7) *Stonehenge.* Official Guide Book (HMSO, London, 1970 ed.; p. 23).

8) Ibid. p. 20.

9) There is no direct evidence that there ever existed a circle or a horseshoe of bluestone trilithons at Stonehenge; but it is certain from the shapes of the stones that at least two bluestone trilithons were built at some time and in some place, and it has been deduced from the results of excavations that at one time there did exist a circle or oval of dressed bluestones in the central area of Stonehenge.

An interesting discovery was made in 1970 when Professor Atkinson found buried in an 'undisturbed context' on the top of Silbury Hill 'a fragment of rock apparently identical with one of the varieties of Stonehenge bluestone (volcanic ash)'. (*Antiquity* vol. 44, p. 314.) If the founder of the Stonehenge colony was buried under Silbury Hill, and if he was the architect of an earlier bluestone temple in Wales, it would be natural for his people to bury a fragment of his great work with him in his tomb. The fact that they buried it in the top of the mound instead of in the burial chamber suggests that the move of the bluestones from Wales was not accomplished until some time after his death. (There is, however, evidence suggesting that *some* bluestones had been brought to Wessex at a very early date, perhaps even before Stonehenge I.)

7 Myths and Magic

EVERY FOURTH year the ancient Greeks held athletic contests at Delphi to celebrate the birth of Apollo, and it was customary for the winners of these contests, like those of the Olympic games, to have their victories commemorated in songs composed by the leading song-writers of the day. In one of these songs the poet Pindar addressed a hymn of praise to 'Hyperborean Apollo'. He described 'the land of the Hyperboreans' as an inaccessible country of perfect happiness. It was a land where beauty and elegance were held in high esteem; where girls danced to the music of lyre and flute with wreathes of golden bayleaves round their hair; where people ate and drank merrily together without fear of want or war; and where sickness and old age were unknown. [1]

This was England, pictured by a Greek poet at the turn of the sixth and fifth centuries BC. Some scholars have denied that this description was anything more than a poetic vision of a purely imaginary paradise. But there is little doubt that the Hyperboreans were real people; and such a vision would scarcely have been associated with their country if they had been cannibals.

Herodotus, 'the father of history', who travelled far and wide over the known world a generation later, made enquiries about the Hyperboreans but failed to find out much about them. The northernmost people he knew, namely the Scythians who lived in Russia and East Europe north of the Danube, had scarcely heard of them. Only the inhabitants of the Aegean island of Delos, famed birthplace of Apollo and sacred centre of that god's religion, were able to tell him anything worth recording. From them Herodotus learnt that the Hyperboreans regularly sent parcels to Delos consisting of 'certain sacred offerings packed in wheat-straw', and the first people they employed as messengers to carry these offerings were girls. [2]

In his monumental *Natural History* written in the first century AD, Pliny the Elder referred to the mild climate of the land of the Hyperboreans, to the godly ways of its peaceful inhabitants, and to their marvellous good health. They only die, he said, when they have lived long enough; then the old folk make good cheer, anoint their bodies with sweet unguents, and jump off 'a certain rock' into the sea.[3] This may sound incredible, like some of the other '20,000 matters of importance' which Pliny recorded in his massive but unoriginal work, until one realises that voluntary euthanasia practised in such a manner would be an entirely logical and sensible custom for a society that firmly believes death to be merely an episode in an endless cycle, leading to rebirth.

The passage in classical literature that enables us positively to identify the Hyperboreans with the inhabitants of Britain occurs in the history of Diodorus of Sicily, who wrote in the time of Augustus but was here quoting from a lost work by Hecataeus of Abdera, a contemporary of Alexander the Great (c. 330 BC). This is the account given by Diodorus.

'Of those who have written about the ancient myths (relating to the Hyperboreans), Hecataeus and certain others say that in the regions beyond the land of the Celts there lies in the ocean an island no smaller than Sicily. This island, the account continues, is situated in the north and is inhabited by the Hyperboreans, who are called by that name because their home is beyond the point whence the north wind (Boreas) blows; and the island is both fertile and productive of every crop, and since it has an unusually temperate climate it produces two harvests each year. Moreover, the following legend is told concerning it: Leto was born on this island, and for that reason Apollo is honoured among them above all other gods; and the inhabitants are looked upon as priests of Apollo, after a manner, since daily they praise this god continuously in song and honour him exceedingly. And there is also on the island both a magnificent sacred precinct of Apollo and a notable temple which is adorned with many votive offerings and is spherical in shape. Furthermore, a city is there which is sacred to this god, and the majority of its inhabitants are players on the cithera; and these continually play on this instrument in the temple and sing hymns of praise to the god, glorifying his deeds.

The Hyperboreans also have a language, we are informed, which is peculiar to them, and are most friendly disposed towards the Greeks, and especially towards the Athenians and the Delians, who have inherited this good-will from most ancient times. The myth also relates that certain Greeks visited the Hyperboreans and left behind them there costly votive offerings bearing inscriptions in Greek letters. And in the same way Abaris, a Hyperborean, came to Greece in ancient times and renewed the good-will and kinship of his people to the Delians. They say also that the moon, as viewed from this island, appears to be but a little distance from the earth and to have upon it prominences, like those of the earth, which are visible to the eye. The account is also given that the god visits the island every nineteen years, the period in which the return of the stars to the same place in the heavens is accomplished; and for this reason the nineteen-year period is called by the Greeks the "year of Meton". At the time of this appearance of the god he both plays on the cithera and dances continuously the night through from the vernal equinox until the rising of the Pleiades, expressing in this manner his delight in his successes. And the kings of this city and the supervisors of the sacred precincts are called Boreades, since they are descendants of Boreas, and the succession to these positions is always kept in their family.'[4]

'The land of the Celts' (or Gauls) clearly means France, so the island can hardly be any other than Britain; and Stonehenge is the only site in Britain where the remains of a pre-Christian structure have been found which could reasonably be identified with the magnificent 'spherical' temple of Apollo. The Greek word translated here as 'spherical in shape' is *sphaero-eides*, which might be translated literally as 'having the appearance of a sphere or ball'. It is not possible without doing violence to the original to translate it, as is sometimes done, 'circular', meaning circular in two dimensions only. In every case where the word occurs in the references given in Liddell and Scott's lexicon it implies circularity in three dimensions. (In Greek, as in English, people sometimes said 'circular' when they meant 'spherical', but they never wrote 'spherical' when they meant 'circular'.) But *sphaero-eides* is sometimes used to describe a *hemispherical* object such as the rounded end of a cylindrical rod or post, and it is in this meaning that the context strongly suggests the word is intended to be used in Hecataeus' description of the temple of Apollo.

On this interpretation we are driven to the conclusion that either the Greek historian was guilty of an error of fact, or Stonehenge was at one time covered by a hemispherical dome. At first sight, the former alternative seems the more probable, but it is never wise to dismiss factual statements in history books as fabrications simply on the ground that they cannot be made to fit in with current theories. The only reason why the idea that the Stonehenge temple might once have had a domed roof has never been seriously entertained is that the construction of a dome would obviously have been beyond the capacity of the neolithic people who are believed to have built the temple.

Once it is conceded that the builders may have been civilized, intelligent, and well-organised people, the roofing of Stonehenge by means of a dome over the whole structure without internal support becomes a practical possibility. Just such a dome was built by the Mormons to roof their Tabernacle in Salt Lake City in the 1860s, when they were hundreds of miles distant from civilization. It is an oval structure 250 ft by 150 ft with no interior pillars, made entirely of wood without the use of metal, even for nails. A dome over Stonehenge would have been easier to build than the Mormon Tabernacle because it would have been circular and smaller, say 140 feet in diameter. In both cases the building would have been carried out largely by unskilled labour inspired by a sense of purpose derived from religious faith.

One piece of archaeological evidence seems at first sight to be consistent with this idea. The 'Y' and 'Z' holes, dug some time after the last of the sarsen stones had been erected, are placed where we might expect to find the foundations of the wooden structure that supported a dome. Atkinson says that the holes were never used to support megaliths, but that does not mean that it can be proved that they could not have held stout wooden pillars like those that were used to support heavy masonry in the Palace of Minos in Cnossos — tree trunks erected upside down, tapering downwards, placed either on a flat stone plinth or directly on solid ground without one.

Apollo, to whom the spherical temple of the Hyperboreans was dedicated, was not only a sun god; he was also a god of healing. Could there be a connection here between the famed good health of those people, the identity of the god they worshipped, and the magic medicinal properties of the stones of the Giants' Ring which the wizard Merlin brought from Ireland in Geoffrey of Monmouth's tale? And could there also be a connection between the technical magic displayed in the erection of the stones and the worship of Apollo in his third capacity as god of technology and the arts?

22. Avebury. *The outer circle of stones is about 1200 feet (370 m.) in diameter, the largest in Britain*

The men whom King Aurelius sent to Ireland, according to Geoffrey, to fetch the stones had first to fight a battle with the Irish.

He continues:

> 'Having won the day, the Britons made their way to Mount Killaraus. When they came to the stone structure, they were filled with joy and wonder. Merlin came up to them as they stood round in a group. "Try your strength, young men", said he, "and see whether skill can do more than brute strength, or strength more than skill, when it comes to dismantling these stones." '

97

'At his bidding they all set to with every conceivable kind of mechanism and strove their hardest to take the Ring down. They rigged up hawsers and ropes and they propped up scaling-ladders, each preparing what he thought most useful, but none of these things advanced them an inch. When he saw what a mess they were making of it, Merlin burst out laughing. He placed in position all the gear which he considered necessary and dismantled the stones more easily than you could ever believe. Once he had pulled them down, he had them carried to the ships and stored on board, and they all set sail once more for Britain with joy in their hearts.'

A ceremony was duly arranged for the burial of the men whose deaths the stones were to commemorate. Then 'Aurelius ordered Merlin to erect round the burial-place the stones which he had brought from Ireland. Merlin obeyed the King's orders and put the stones up in a circle round the sepulchre, in exactly the same way as they had been arranged on Mount Killaraus in Ireland, thus proving that his artistry was worth more than any brute strength.'[5]

Both in Egypt and in Bronze Age Greece huge blocks of stone weighing many tons were used in building construction. There is no technical reason why the builders should not have been able to invent cranes to lift them, but we have no records of any such machines having been used; in fact, the evidence regarding the pyramids indicates that the Egyptians did not use these machines. There are, however, references in Greek myths to fabulous monsters called 'Cyclopses'. These near-human giants were supposed to have built the so-called 'Cyclopean' walls of Tiryns and Mycenae the stones of which were thought too heavy to have been lifted by ordinary mortals. The name 'Cyclops' was interpreted by the Greeks themselves as meaning 'one-eyed', but a more literal translation might be 'wheel-faced'. This would be an entirely apt description of a crane built on the 'wheel and axle' principle — the first form of mechanical lifting tackle that is likely to have been invented.

It is perfectly possible that Egyptians in remote and uncivilized Britain, faced with challenges that had never been encountered in the ancient and strictly regulated culture of the Old Kingdom, broke away from their conservative traditions to develop new techniques, and that later on they exported the fruits of their inventive enterprise to the vigorous young civilizations that were then growing up in the Aegean. In that case, the Mycenaean architect whom Professor Atkinson imagined, on the strength of the axe and dagger carvings on the sarsen stones, as having come to Britain from Greece to teach Wessex people how to build a temple for their chief, may have come not to teach but to learn. Perhaps he was an architect-priest of Apollo who came with Delian gold to help the impoverished priests of Stonehenge to rebuild their decaying temple, and to learn in the course of that work the ingenious methods their forebears had devised long ago for accomplishing feats of strength which were still impossible in his own country.

From this interchange of ideas there could have developed a practice whereby Aegean architects who were required to build fortress palaces for Mycenaean kings came to Britain to hire teams of British craftsmen with their 'cyclops' cranes. In the astonished eyes of the ordinary Greek people, these gigantic wheel-faced machines, which had been dismantled for the voyage and re-assembled on the site, and which they saw from a distance lifting 20-ton blocks of stone high into the air, would have appeared like giants from outer space — giants even more nearly human than the first railway locomotives that were imported into southern Greece from British workshops in the last century. There are people alive today who can recall hearing from eye-witnesses how, when the first steam locomotive appeared at the port of Kalamata and was about to set off on its first journey through the Peloponnese, peasants came in from the country bringing bundles of corn and hay which they laid on the ground in front of the fire-breathing monster. They wanted to make sure that it had a good meal before it left and would not be tempted to wander off its track into their fields in search of food.

Magic of a less spectacular but humanly more beneficial kind was practised by the Egyptians, we suggest, in the field of medicine. It is central to our theme that the priests of Ra-Harakhte were, first and foremost, scientists. If they believed in a god at all, as we are sure they did, that god was not the sun itself but the intelligent being who created the sun and who set the earth spinning round it in such a miraculous and evidently purposeful manner that all the myriad conditions that are essential for the support of intelligent life were satisfied. The god that these men worshipped was, in effect, the Divine Intelligence, and it made no difference whether they named him Ra or Horus or Apollo. The method of their worship was the same at all times, namely to practice the exercise of their own intelligences to the fullest extent of their capacity; for imitation is the sincerest form of praise. That is why they were mathematicians, scientists, and engineers.

If such men came to Britain to study the motions of heavenly bodies and if they set up their first observatory at a certain spot in South Wales (because that was the only place they could find that was both at the right latitude and also within easy reach of the sea) one can understand why they decided later to move. Men who have lived all their lives under the perpetually clear skies of Africa can be excused for not appreciating that in more northern latitudes climatic conditions are an important factor to be taken into account when siting an observatory. Not until after some years of frustrated endeavour would the priest-scientists have realised that their task was hopeless. The clouds that brood for weeks on end over the Welsh mountains seldom lifted at the few critical moments in the year when the full moon was about to rise or set.

On Salisbury Plain the skies are clearer, and systematic observations would have been possible. But even in a perfect climate astronomers cannot spend all day looking at the sky or making calculations from previous nights' observations. Assuming that the colony as a whole was big enough to provide the basic necessities and comforts of life, the inner circle of initiates would have needed some more continuous field of study to keep them occupied. What better field could be found than that of medical research? The fruits of such studies would not only be valuable for improving the standard of health of their own people; they could also be used in demonstrations of healing magic to impress the natives with the marvellous extent of the newcomers' divine powers and so ensure the continuance of peaceful relations between the two widely disparate racial communities.

It would be surprising if in the course of many centuries of assiduous research, even with very limited facilities at their disposal, a group of dedicated scientists had not made significant progress in analysing the causes of diseases and in finding remedies. The proverbial good health of the Hyperboreans could be an indication of such progress. The stories told about them by the Greeks may, of course, be purely fictitious, but we think it more likely that they were founded, like most ancient myths, on some basis of fact.

More specific evidence is traceable in the person of Abaris, the Hyperborean priest who is referred to in the passage from Diodorus quoted above as having come to Greece 'in ancient times and renewed the good-will and kinship of his people to the Delians'. A translator's footnote to this passage says that 'Abaris is apparently a purely mythical figure who in some authors sailed on his arrow, as on a witch's broomstick, through the air over rivers and seas.' Similar tales of Abaris' magic powers had reached Herodotus, but tantalisingly he did not pass them on. 'I will not tell', he says, 'the tale of Abaris, a Hyperborean who is supposed to have gone all round the world carrying an arrow and never eating anything.'

The father of history passed on many tall stories which he picked up in the course of his travels, but the stories of Abaris the magician were too tall even for him.

Classical historians traditionally dismiss tales of magic as unworthy of scholarly attention, but to us any mention of a witch's broomstick or a wizard's wand evokes the smell of the scientist's laboratory. Although Abaris is a shadowy mythical character, there are too many references to him in classical literature for us to suppose that he never existed. The date of his visit to Greece is assigned to the sixth century BC. He is said to have cured diseases by incantations and delivered whole communities from plagues; and it seems that charms and potions bearing his name commanded a high price for a long time after his visit.

Our suggestion is that Abaris the magician was in fact the last descendant of the long line of Egyptian priest-scientists who founded Stonehenge and who kept the torch of the ancient wisdom burning for twenty centuries while the civilization of the Bronze Age rose and fell and that of the Iron Age sprang from its ruins. We claim support for this view from the following account by the Neoplatonist philosopher Iamblichus of a meeting between Abaris and the Greek mathematician Pythagoras (c. 580-500 BC). Pythagoras had acquired world fame not only as a mathematician and natural philosopher but also as a divinely inspired worker of miracles. He was especially famed for his alleged possession of a golden thigh, which was supposed to constitute visible proof of his divine nature. Our quotation is taken from a chapter of Iamblichus' *Life of Pythagoras* (c. AD 300) describing the teaching methods applied by the Master for the initiation of his pupils into the secret mysteries of the Pythagorean philosophy and religion.

'When Abaris the Scythian [6] came from the Hyperboreans, he was already of an advanced age, and unskilled and uninitiated in the Greek learning. Pythagoras did not compel him to wade through introductory theorems, the period of silence, and long auscultation, not to mention other trials, but considered him to be fit for an immediate listener to his doctrines, and instructed him in the shortest way in his treatises On Nature, and the one On the Gods.

This Hyperborean Abaris was elderly, and most wise in sacred concerns, being a priest of the Apollo there worshipped. At that time he was returning from Greece to his country, in order to consecrate the gold which he had collected to the God in his temple among the Hyperboreans. As therefore he was passing through Italy, he saw Pythagoras, and identified him as the God of whom he was the priest.

Believing that Pythagoras resembled no man, but was none other than the God himself, Apollo, both from the venerable associations he saw around him, and from those the priest already knew, he paid him homage by giving him a sacred dart. This dart he had taken with him when he had left his temple, as an implement that would stand him in good stead in the difficulties that might befall him in so long a journey. For in passing through inaccessible places, such as rivers, lakes, marshes, mountains, and the like, it carried him, and by it he was said to have performed lustrations and expelled winds and pestilences from the cities that requested him to liberate them from such evils. For instance, it was said that Lacedemon, after having been by him purified, was no longer infected with pestilence, which formerly had been endemic through the miasmatic nature of the ground, in the suffocating heat produced by the overhanging mountain Taygetus, just as happens with Cnossus in Crete. Many other similar circumstances were reported of Abaris.

Pythagoras, however, accepted the dart, without expressing any amazement at the novelty of the thing, nor asking why the dart was presented to him, as if he really was a god. Then he took Abaris aside and showed him his golden thigh as an indication that he was not wholly mistaken (in his estimate of his real nature). Then Pythagoras described to him several details of his distant

Hyperborean temple, as proof of deserving being considered divine. He advised Abaris to stay with him, to aid him in correcting (the manners and morals) of those they might meet, and to share the common resources of himself and his associates, whose reason led them to practice the precept that the *possessions of friends are common.*

So Abaris stayed with him, and was compendiously taught physiology and theology . . . and other studies for which he was fit.' [7]

It may be objected that the apparent credulity of the author of this passage in accepting obviously mythical accounts of impossible feats of magic rule him out as a credible recorder of true events. But Iamblichus was no fool; he was a wise man and a philosopher of no mean repute. True to the tradition of wise men of ancient times he never gave away another wise man's secret. If he knew a truth that another was trying to conceal he kept it to himself. What the reader therefore must do with Iamblichus, as with Plato in his myths, is not to reject him but to read between the lines. From the information he has given, we are entitled to conclude that Abaris was a medical practitioner of no mean skill.

In another passage Iamblichus states clearly that Abaris 'came from the Hyperborean regions in order that he might collect gold for his temple.' [8] It is reasonable to infer from this that the temple at Stonehenge was in urgent need of very extensive repairs. South Italy, where Pythagoras was then teaching in the city of Croton, enjoyed a reputation for wealth and liberality equivalent to that of North America today. The idea of setting out for America to collect funds for a temple in need of repair is surely one that will strike a sympathetic chord in the minds of many a dean and chapter of Gothic cathedrals in England today.

The fact that Abaris remained with Pythagoras in Italy instead of returning to England is significant. If our interpretation of the beliefs of the priests of Ra-Harakhte is correct, and they were astronomer-mathematicians who saw in the recurrent risings and settings of the stars a model of the recurrent human cycle of birth, death, and re-birth, then one can understand the joy of the old priest from the barbarian north at finding this wise and kindly Greek, who held exactly the same beliefs as himself, actually controlling through the Pythagorean brotherhoods he had established, the administration of several of the richest and most civilized cities in the world. Small wonder that Abaris made him a gift of his own most precious possession and decided to spend the rest of his days under Pythagoras' benevolent tutelage in Croton.

The name *Abaris* may also have some significance for our theory, for it has an Egyptian ring about it. There was a city in the Nile Delta in the extreme north of Egypt called Avaris,[9] where the name apparently means 'temple of the district'. In an inscription dating from the time of Queen Hatshepsut the city is referred to as 'Avaris of the Northland'. Perhaps the equivalent English name of our Hyperborean priest might be 'Lord Northchurch'.

It would seem not unlikely that the original Egyptian colonists named their first settlement in Britain after the town in the north of Egypt, and that the high priest and ruler took his title from the town. This might offer a better explanation for the kings referred to by Diodorus being called 'Boreades' than is offered by that historian's theory that they were so called because they were descended from Boreas, the north wind. It might also explain the origin of the name 'Britain' itself, the root of 'Abaris' in Greek being 'Abarid-'. Geoffrey of Monmouth derives the name from a mythical hero called 'Brutus' who he says came from Troy and was the first man to bring civilization to Britain, as Aeneas did to Rome. This suggests an ancient tradition still extant in Wales in the 12th century AD that the first seeds of British civilized culture were planted here by immigrants from the eastern Mediterranean.

Notes on Chapter 7

1) Pindar, *Pythian Odes* x, 50-55.

2) Herodotus iv, 36.

3) Pliny, *Natural History*, iv, 89. The 'certain rock' could, we suggest, have been Beachy Head, and the 'unguents' could have been analgesic creams intended to deaden any momentary pain.

4) Diodorus Siculus ii, 47. Trans. C. H. Oldfather (The Loeb Classical Library, Harvard University Press: William Heinemann). 'The year of Meton' refers to the 'Metonic cycle' of 19 years; named after the Athenian astronomer of the fifth century BC who discovered that 235 lunar months are almost exactly equal to 19 solar years and therefore the full moons occur on the same calendar dates at the same point in each cycle.

5) Geoffrey of Monmouth, *The History of the Kings of Britain* viii 12. Trans. Lewis Thorpe (Penguin Books, London,1966).

6) For Mediterranean people of the ancient world the distinction between Scythians from the mainland and the islander Hyperboreans must have been about as hard to draw as the distinction between Chinese and Japanese was for medieval Europeans.

7) Iamblichus, *De Vita Pythagorae*, xix. Trans. K. S. Guthrie.

8) Loc. cit. xxviii.

9) There is no letter 'v' in ancient Greek.

8 Archaeologists and Astronomers

NOT ONLY the orientation of Stonehenge towards the midsummer sunrise, but also the circular lay-out and the clear-cut vertical and horizontal lines of its stones have suggested to observers in the past that its primary function was the making of astronomical observations. (A large multi-storey circular stone structure with rectangular apertures was built for this purpose in India by the Maharajah of Jaipur in the eighteenth century AD.) In 1902 Sir Norman Lockyer, then Astronomer Royal, developed the idea in some detail and used the exact alignment of the axis to calculate the date at which Stonehenge was built, which he put at 1680 BC. He believed that, like certain sun-oriented structures of the East, Stonehenge was designed as a calendar for agricultural purposes to enable precise dates to be determined in the year for ploughing and sowing. But it was not until the last decade that any systematic attempt was made to substantiate the 'observatory theory' with more detailed measurements and calculations.

Early in 1963 Mr. C. A. Newham, an amateur astronomer, published in the *Yorkshire Post* a brief account of the results of several years' study of the possible astronomical significance of the alignments of some of the stones at Stonehenge. A full account of these important findings was given the following year in a booklet published by himself under the title *The Enigma of Stonehenge and its Astronomical and Geometrical Significance*. His conclusions fully supported Lockyer's diagnosis. 'There is not the slightest reason', he wrote, 'to depart from the belief that the outlying features of Stonehenge were ingeniously arranged in order to provide a calendar by which the religious and social activities of the peoples concerned could be arranged'.

Meanwhile a more detailed study was being undertaken by an American astronomer, Dr. Gerald S. Hawkins, Professor of Astronomy at Boston University. Professor Hawkins plotted the positions of what he regarded as all the significant stones and stone-holes, fed them into a computer, and used the computer to calculate the declinations (i.e. the angular distances from the celestial equator) of the points in the sky to which straight lines joining pairs of positions would point on the horizon when viewed from either end. There were 165 positions giving 27,060 possible alignments, from which Hawkins and his collaborators chose 120 alignments as the most likely to be significant, i.e. the most likely to have been actually intended to be used as sight lines, judging by the distances between the stones or stone holes and their positions relative to one another.

If the stones had all been placed by the builders without regard to astronomical considerations one would expect the computer's print-out to show a more or less random distribution of declinations having no correlation with the declinations of celestial bodies. But instead, 'we noticed at once', says Hawkins, 'that among the declinations which the machine had produced there was a large number of duplications. Figures approximating + (north) 29°, +24° and + 19° and their southern counterparts —29°, —24° and —19° occurred frequently. We decided to see what celestial bodies were close to those declinations.'

Strangely, the astronomers checked first on the stars and planets to see which of them would have matched these positions in 1500 BC, the date they assumed for the building of Stonehenge. Only when this exercise produced a negative result did they try the most obvious bodies, the sun and moon. This time, allowing for a small margin of error, the fit was complete. In 1500 BC the sun swung between maximum declinations of +23°.9 at midsummer and —23°.9 at midwinter, and the moon's orbit oscillated in a cycle of 18.61 years between two maxima of plus and minus 29°.0 and 18°.7.

In other words, the builders of Stonehenge had, either by design or accident, placed their stones in such a way that several pairs of them could be used as directional sight lines to line up with the extreme positions reached by the sun and moon in the periodic motions of their points of rising and setting along the horizon. Hawkins found that there were 24 of these significant directions (some lines he counted as giving two directions, one each way). Of these 24, 16 (8 pointing to the sun and 8 to the moon) were from pairs of positions supposedly dating from Stonehenge I and the remaining 8 (4 sun and 4 moon) from Stonehenge III.

Among the Stonehenge I positions he included the four 'station stones' which are set in a rectangle on the circumference of the Aubrey hole circle. The short sides of the rectangle are

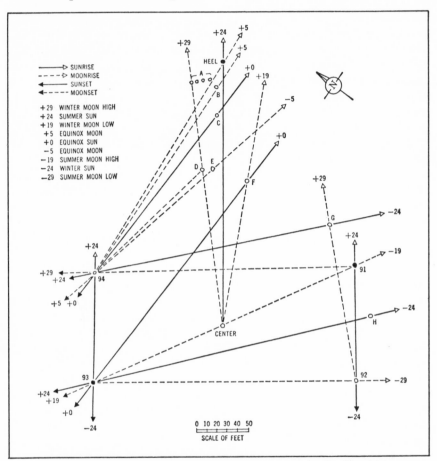

23. *Significant astronomical alignments found by Dr Hawkins*

parallel with the axis of Stonehenge and point to midsummer sunrise and midwinter sunset, while the long sides, Hawkins discovered, point to midsummer moonrise and midwinter moonset at their *greatest* declinations. The relative lengths of these lines was so chosen that one of the diagonals passing through the centre of the circle points one way to midsummer moonrise and the other to midwinter moonset at their *least* declinations.

A further remarkable point about the station stones is that the sun and moon alignments given by the sides of the rectangle would not be at right angles to one another at any latitude markedly different from that of Stonehenge. Forty miles or so further north or further south the angles between the lines would have to be at least one degree greater or less than a right angle. Hawkins drew the inference that the site of Stonehenge was deliberately chosen with this in mind. The practical advantage offered by a rectangle is that a circle enclosing it will be smaller than that enclosing a non-rectangular parallelogram having sides of equal length. In other words, given that a group of astronomers had decided to place four stones in a quadrilateral in such a way that the four sides and one diagonal pointed to the extreme sun and moon positions indicated by the Stonehenge station stones; and if they also had to build a rampart and a ditch encircling the quadrilateral to protect themselves against the attacks of barbarians, and for economic or military reasons wanted to make that circle as small as possible, they could not have chosen a better site than the one actually chosen by the founders of Stonehenge.

The correlations found by Hawkins between the alignments of the stones and the calculated positions of the sun and moon were not, of course, exact. There were discrepancies or errors of varying magnitude, and these he discussed at some length. These errors are of the utmost importance to the 'observatory theory' because on them depends the whole of the argument that is based on probability. If the twenty-four alignments only fitted the calculated directions within a broad margin of, say, plus or minus five degrees there would be a strong probability that the correlation was due to chance. If on the other hand they were all exact to a hundredth of a degree one could say there was almost total certainty that the alignments were intentional.

Assuming that the alignments were intentional, errors would have arisen from a number of different causes. The builders themselves might have positioned the stones inaccurately; the stones have been weathered and have tilted or moved over the centuries; some have disappeared altogether and uncertainty exists regarding the exact original positions of their centres. Some errors noted by Hawkins may be due to the use of inaccurate site data. Or the calculated position of the sun and moon may be wrong due to his wrong choice of date (1500 BC), or to wrong assumptions about the level of the visible horizon at that date, or to a wrong assumption on the question whether the stones were intended to be aligned with the first gleam of the rising orb and the last gleam of its setting, or with the positions at the moment when the whole orb stood tangentially on the horizon, or with a position midway between the two when exactly half the orb was visible.

Some of these errors can be estimated and specifically allowed for, others not. After making such allowances wherever he could, Hawkins found that the resultant discrepancies between actual and calculated lines showed a significant pattern in two respects. First, the biggest errors were in respect of lines formed by stones which had fallen down and been re-erected in modern times. Secondly, in 10 out of the 12 moon lines the error was on the side one would expect it to be on if the full moon had been obscured by cloud on the few nights in the 18½ year cycle when it reached the extreme limit of its travel, and the builders had consequently marked a position just short of that limit.

Professor Hawkins first published the results of these studies in an article in *Nature* in October 1963. He received as a result many letters, in one of which a suggestion was made that caused him to extend his computer exercise to take into account three outlying stone holes which he had previously ignored. These, together with one already included (all four supposedly dating from Stonehenge I) yielded eight more significant directions pointing to critical points of the sun's and moon's orbits — not, this time, extreme points reached at the solstices but midpoints reached at the equinoxes. Two pairs of stones pointed to the solar equinoctial positions, i.e. due east and west (giving 4 directions). The other four directions pointed to the moon's equinoctial positions, three at its highest declination and one at its lowest.

Using probability theory Hawkins calculated that the chances of 24 alignments being produced by accident even within a margin of error as wide as ±2° — a margin wider than that of all the errors he had actually found except one — were over 10,000 to 1 against. When the Stonehenge III alignments were also taken into account the probability fell to 10,000,000 to 1 against.

Not the least remarkable fact that emerged was that Stonehenge III was built in such a way that it avoided obscuring any of the Stonehenge I sight lines despite the lapse of several centuries and the intervening supersession of one local Stone Age culture by another.

Speculating on the builders' motives, the only practical purpose that Hawkins could see at first was that proposed by Sir Norman Lockyer, namely, to create a calendar for the determination of the seasons for agricultural operations. But later it occurred to him that the stones could have been used to give warning of solar and lunar eclipses. He argued that in a cycle of approximately 56 years made of three periods of 18.61 years each (the period of revolution of the lunar nodes) the pattern of eclipses recurs, and he suggested that the 56 Aubrey holes were used to house markers that were moved round the circle year by year in such a way that from their positions the Stonehenge priests could tell roughly when to expect the possibility of an eclipse that year. The suggestion was published in a second article in *Nature*, but the theory behind it was not accepted by other astronomers. It remains of interest nevertheless because it appears to be the first suggestion ever made that has attempted, albeit unsuccessfully, to offer a mathematical explanation for the mysterious fact that the Aubrey holes are 56 in number. It was also the jumping off point for a more sophisticated 'eclipse prediction' theory presently to be put forward by Professor Hoyle.

The full account of Hawkins' theory and findings was published in his popular book *Stonehenge Decoded* in 1965.[1] Although, or perhaps because, Professor Hawkins' ideas when first expounded in *Nature* had aroused widespread attention in many countries and his conclusions had been accepted unquestioningly by large sections of the lay public, this noisy intrusion by an American astronomer into the sequestered field of British prehistory was greeted by the local archaeological fraternity with a welcome that was something less than friendly. In a withering review in *Nature* under the heading 'Decoder Misled', Professor Atkinson was severely critical of the book's failures to comply with the rigorous standards demanded of a scientific enquiry, particularly in its 'slipshod' treatment of some of the archaeological data, and he concluded that, as an attempt to substantiate its author's claim that Stonehenge was an observatory, the book was a failure.[2]

In a subsequent more detailed review in the archaeological journal *Antiquity* under the heading 'Moonshine on Stonehenge', Professor Atkinson slated not only Hawkins' archaeological mistakes but also his calculations. He claimed that a correct calculation using more objective input data showed that the chances of 23 alignments — the number actually found by Hawkins for Stonehenge I within his (arbitrary) margin of error of $\pm 2°$ — occurring accidentally were not, as Hawkins had claimed, more than 10,000 to 1 against but more like 32 to 1 in favour, or at worst about even, depending on how many *possibly* significant alignments there exist between pairs of stones or stone-holes. Hawkins put this number, apparently arbitrarily, at 50, but Atkinson made it at least 111 and perhaps as many as 159.

The archaeologist also rejected on archaeological grounds the astronomer's idea that the Aubrey holes were dug merely to house movable markers. 'If you want to establish a set of *permanent* tally-marks which will be usable over a number of cycles of 56 years each, to dig a ring of 56 pits and then immediately to fill them up is perhaps a rather curious way of going about it. Excavation leaves no doubt that the Aubrey holes *were* filled up very soon after they were dug.'[3]

Meanwhile, Professor Fred Hoyle, who held the chair of Astronomy and Experimental Philosophy in the University of Cambridge, had entered the lists on the side of his fellow astronomer. He re-worked all the alignments found by Hawkins and expressed the opinion that the arrangement was not random. 'As Hawkins points out', he said, 'some positions are specially relevant in relation to the geometrical regularities of Stonehenge, and it is these particular positions that show the main alignments. Furthermore, I find these alignments are just the ones that could have served far-reaching astronomical purposes.'[4]

Hoyle had been asked for his opinion on Hawkins' astronomical conclusions by Dr. Glyn Daniel, the distinguished archaeologist-editor of *Antiquity*, himself the author of important works on the megalithic culture, who now proceeded to conduct a debate between the two sides in the pages of that journal. Hoyle developed his theory in considerable detail. The method he used to tackle the astronomical problem was essentially the same as that which had been used by the archaeologists to tackle the engineering and transport problems. He asked himself the questions: if we twentieth century people with our brains and our knowledge but without any of our modern equipment had set out to do what the builders of Stonehenge apparently succeeded in doing, how would we have set about doing it? To answer this question, he imagined himself waking up on another planet where the periodic motions of sun and moon are different from what they are here, and asked himself how he would set out to discover the properties of that solar system using only sticks and stones and string.

The answer, he concluded, was to build a structure just like

Stonehenge — more particularly, like Stonehenge I. The arguments he used to support this conclusion were highly technical. They embraced no less than 28 equations in plane and spherical trigonometry. But these equations made his argument less rather than more convincing. The more complicated the astronomy the more impossible it seemed that it could have been understood by the Stone Age people of Britain in the twentieth century BC. Hoyle himself admitted that the argument 'not only requires Stonehenge to have been constructed as an astronomical instrument but it demands a level of intellectual attainment orders of magnitude higher than the standard to be expected from a community of primitive farmers. A veritable Newton or Einstein must have been at work. But then, why not?'[5]

Why not indeed? There is no known biological reason why a genius might not have been born to ordinary parents in such a community; but there are a great many reasons why, if a Newton or an Einstein had been so born, he would have achieved nothing at all unless he had been, impossibly, a Napoleon as well. If a genius *was* at work it must have been as a member of a community of highly intelligent men whose practical skills extended far beyond farming.

Professor Hoyle was particularly impressed by Hawkins' argument based on 'the sign of the errors'. He found it extremely improbable that such a large majority of the moon lines (10 out of 12) should have erred by accident on the side where they fell short of the limit of the moon's travel along the horizon, but he attributed these errors not to difficulties of observation experienced by the builders but to their deliberate intention. He thought their purpose was to determine with more certainty than could be done by a marker at the extreme limit (where the moon hovers for a few days before reversing its motion) the exact moment at which it reached that limit. (We think that Hawkins' simpler explanation is the more probable but the question is not a material one. What matters is that the errors have a rational explanation and are not random.)

On the purpose of the Aubrey holes Hoyle accepted Hawkins' basic idea that they were intended to hold markers and that the number 56 was related to the period of revolution of the lunar nodes. But he thought the equal divisions of the circle showed it was meant to be used as a protractor representing the circle of the ecliptic, and he put forward an ingenious theory showing how, with additional markers for the sun and moon, it could

113

have been used for the prediction of eclipses. But Atkinson's objections to Hawkins' theory are equally valid against Hoyle's.

An apparently even more damaging objection to the eclipse prediction theory came from another astronomer, Mr. D. H. Sadler, Superintendent of H.M. Nautical Almanac Office, Royal Greenwich Observatory. Sadler pointed out that the theory pre-supposed that the designers already knew before they started to build that there was a causal connection between the occurrence of eclipses and the directions of the risings and settings of the sun and moon, although the existence of this connection could only have been established by careful observation and record-keeping over a period of years. Climatic conditions which rendered many eclipses invisible would not have favoured the keeping of such records in Britain even if the Stone Age inhabitants of the country had been capable of doing so.

Since the keeping of records of eclipses demands an ability to read and write and the possession of an accurate calendar, Sadler's argument is conclusive against Stonehenge having been built for eclipse prediction by illiterate barbarians. But it is not conclusive against the theory that it was built for this purpose by educated men. What it does is to point strongly to the conclusion that, if it *was* built as an astronomical observatory, it was built by men who already knew from centuries of recorded observations elsewhere (probably in a sunnier climate) that eclipses are predictable from calculations of the motions of the sun and moon based on accurate observations and records.

A more promising suggestion was made by Mr. C. A. Newham in an article in *Nature* in July 1966. This is interesting as the only suggestion yet made that holds out hope that the date of the founding of Stonehenge may one day be determined accurately by astronomical means. It concerns the group of about 40 post-holes situated in the Avenue near the north-east entrance.

> 'The holes seem to radiate from the centre of the Aubrey circle and lie within a $10°$ arc north of the heelstone or solstice line. They are roughly arranged into six ranks crossing the line of the causeway. Preliminary calculations reveal that the causeway post-holes lie within the arc or sector of the most northerly limits of winter full-moon-rise as seen from the centre of the Aubrey circle; also the number of holes in any one rank does not exceed the number of risings that could appear north of the heelstone or solstice line in any one cycle (of 18.61 years).'

It is reasonable to infer that over a period of 5½ lunar node cycles, or just over 100 years, observations were made of the rising of the full moon nearest the winter solstice and a stake was planted in the ground to mark the line joining the moon's position on the horizon to the centre of the Aubrey circle. A fresh mark was set up every time that this line appeared north of the solstice line, and the stakes were arranged in rows, one for each cycle. After this century of observations had satisfied the astronomers that they had accurately determined the extreme limit of the moon's travel, seeing that the six northernmost stakes were all in line with one another, they placed a megalith (stone 'D') to mark that line permanently.

Newham hoped that the years when these observations were made could be established by a correlation between the actual positions of all the post-holes with the calculated positions of winter full-moon-rise over a whole century — positions which vary from year to year according to the dates of the full moon. But at the time he wrote all the necessary data for such a correlation to be established had not been worked out. However, a sample calculation carried out by Hawkins on his computer for the period 1814 to 1712 BC showed a good enough fit to make it appear extremely likely that the post-holes were dug for the purpose suggested.

While astronomers were thus at work finding new points of astronomical significance in the Stonehenge layout, archaeologists were busy belittling the significance of those that had already been found. Some of the stone holes used in Hawkins' alignments were called in question on the grounds that they had not been fully enough excavated or that they were probably not man-made holes. In this way 11 out of Hawkins' 23 Stonehenge I alignments were pronounced doubtful. The consequences on the probability calculations were not worked out.

Throughout this controversy the owners of the site and guardians of the public interest, the Ministry of Public Building and Works, remained silent. No impartial mathematician without a theory of his own to put forward was called in to weigh the evidence and estimate the chances for and against Stonehenge having been designed primarily as an astronomical observatory. It fell instead to a member of one of the disputant professions to sum up and pronounce judgment on the dispute. The editor of *Antiquity* entrusted this task to his fellow archaeologist, Jacquetta Hawkes.

Dr. Glyn Daniel's choice of referee was a good one only on the supposition that its object was to ensure that the home side won. Not only was Jacquetta Hawkes a professional archaeologist without any noted aptitude for mathematics but she had already publicly committed herself some years previously to the assertion that 'every age has the Stonehenge it deserves or desires', meaning that in a scientific age Stonehenge will inevitably be viewed as a scientific monument regardless of whether or not it had any scientific meaning for its builders. By recalling this assertion at the beginning of her article, entitled *God in the Machine*, she prepared the reader for the inevitable conclusion at the end: 'I see no argument strong or consistent enough to change our previous belief that Stonehenge was intended primarily as a sanctuary . . . that what went on there was mainly ritualistic and not intellectual. I believe that the orientation was intended to express a religious symbolism just as the orientation of Christian churches expressed a symbolism. I feel that we should show that this is indeed the scientific age by refusing to give way to our own form of wishful thinking.'[6]

A scientific age requires more than not giving way to wishful thinking. It requires an objective examination of the evidence, and this Jacquetta Hawkes failed to provide. Her article was not a judicious appraisal of the possible significance of the undoubted new discoveries made by Hawkins in regard to the astronomical properties of the Stonehenge layout, so much as a partial attempt to refute the astronomical arguments that did not fit in with what she called 'the historic evidence' — i.e. with the conventional archaeological theory that Stonehenge I was built by the contemporaneous neolithic barbarians. Thus, she would have it that the Aubrey holes were no more than primitive burial pits, 'a ring of large and quite irregularly formed holes.' She was silent about Hawkins' description of their spacing: 'a very accurately measured circle 288 feet in diameter with a 16-foot interval between their centre points. The greatest radial error was 19 inches and the greatest circumferential or interval-spacing error was 21 inches. Let it be noted that such accurate spacing of 56 points around the circumference of so large a circle was no mean engineering feat.'

Similarly ignored was the evidence of the two groups of moon alignments and the improbability of the errors being purely accidental.

In listing numerous detailed criticisms of points made by Hawkins, Jacquetta Hawkes was sometimes less than fair. Referring to the passage in Diodorus' History quoted above (pp. 94-95), she took him to task for not knowing 'that it is not even certain that the island of the Hyperboreans is Britain, and that the adjective applied to the temple is usually translated "circular" rather than "spherical".' On the first point, Hawkins gave a full and fair account of the mythical character of the Hyperboreans in classical literature. The second point we have already dealt with (p. 95). (Hawkins had endorsed the rather lame suggestion that by 'spherical in shape', Diodorus meant 'spherical in use', i.e. used for observing the heavenly sphere.) It is a pity the learned judge did not hear expert witnesses before delivering judgement on this point.

Despite the evident bias of Jacquetta Hawkes' summing up it may be agreed that her main conclusion was right, namely that the case so far presented for regarding Stonehenge as a structure designed primarily to serve an astronomical purpose was not strong enough to justify its claim to supplant the accepted archaeological theory that it was built for religious purposes. But the balance of argument was by no means as decisive as the archaeologists made out. Concentration on the weaknesses of the astronomers' case served to distract attention from the weaknesses of their own.

No explanation has been offered to show why, at that early date, people in Britain should decide to worship their gods in a circular building of gigantic stones instead of in simpler structures better suited to the times. Nor has any evidence been adduced to prove the underlying assumption that because Stonehenge and other megalithic structures were built at a time when Britain was inhabited by barbarian people, therefore these structures must have been built by the hands of those people and for their purposes. This is a doctrine which states, in effect, that the phenomenon of two or more peoples of different racial origins and levels of culture living together side by side (though common throughout historical times), could not have occurred in a prehistoric age.

At least Professor Atkinson was conscious of the difference between what is known of the primitive level of the local culture of Britain and the sophisticated methods that must have been used by the builders of Stonehenge when he pointed out a number of parallels between the Stonehenge architecture (notably Stonehenge III) and that practised by the Mycenaeans (for example the use of mortice-and-tenon joints to hold in place the lintels of the great trilithons, a method very similar to that used in the Postern Gate at Mycenae) and put forward his suggestion that a wandering Mycenaean architect might have found employment with a Wessex chieftain.

The apparently solid archaeological front was thus already beginning to crack when Hawkins made his intrusion. Though the manner of that intrusion appeared only to consolidate the front, it did in fact widen the cracks. Professor Atkinson conceded that the builders of Stonehenge had shown that 'they possessed a good deal of empirical knowledge of observational astronomy'. He even accepted that the 'positions at least of the Heel Stone and the Station Stones, and indeed the latitude of Stonehenge itself, were astronomically determined'.

In admitting that the site might have been chosen for its latitude Professor Atkinson appeared not to realise that he was thereby surrendering the whole case for maintaining that the builders were illiterate; for it implied that they knew that the Earth was round. That knowledge, and the ability to use it to determine with reasonable accuracy the latitude of a place on the Earth's surface, could only have been acquired initially by men who had leisure enough to undertake a long and systematic study of the heavens and were equipped with measuring and recording instruments such as no uncivilized community could conceivably invent for themselves.

Late in 1967, at the very time when Jacquetta Hawkes' article was appearing in *Antiquity*, the conventional archaeological theory that she was defending received another shattering blow. In a slim volume [7] packed with facts and figures of unimpeachable accuracy, Alexander Thom, formerly Professor of Engineering in the University of Oxford but then living in retirement in his native Scotland, claimed that a detailed statistical analysis of a vast amount of material obtained by him from accurate surveys of some 600 other megalithic sites in Britain showed conclusively that the designers of those structures had aligned their stones with the extreme and mid positions of sun and moon, and also of certain first magnitude stars, with an accuracy that often attained 1 minute of arc. This is an accuracy 120 times greater than the ±2 degrees postulated by Hawkins as a suitable criterion of significance at Stonehenge, and five times greater than the degree of accuracy which Professor Atkinson found by experiment could actually be obtained with a pair of sighting sticks.

Further, Thom found to his own astonishment that his analysis of the sight lines given by the stones revealed not only that the builders had succeeded in capturing the four extremes of the moon's 18.6 year cycle of plus and minus 19° and 29° declination, but they had even identified the small perturbation to which the moon's orbit is subject on account of the gravitational attraction of the sun.

An eclipse of the sun occurs whenever the moment of a new moon coincides with one of the moon's nodes, that is to say with one of the moments when the moon in its orbit round the earth cuts through the plane of the earth's orbit round the sun (the plane of the ecliptic). The plane of the moon's orbit lies at an angle of about 5° to the ecliptic, but this angle is not constant. It is subject to this slight 'perturbation' or wobble. The amplitude of the wobble is less than ±9 minutes of arc (0°.15) — an amount so small as to be undiscernible except by meticulously accurate observations; but since the angular distance from one of its extremes to the other is about two thirds of that of the sun's diameter and the sun is only eclipsed when it is at a maximum it is vitally necessary to take it into account for the accurate prediction of eclipses.

Thom observed in passing that the effect of the wobble 'would show up in the movement of the setting moon along the horizon, *especially in northern latitudes* (our italics) where the path of the setting moon at its lowest declination makes a very small angle with the horizon'.[8] But he drew no conclusion from this pregnant observation except the general one that the builders of the megalithic circles were concerned with the prediction of eclipses. 'To early man the eclipse of the sun or of the moon must have been an impressive spectacle, and a desire to master eclipse prediction probably motivated Megalithic man's preoccupation with lunar phenomena.'

This is the nearest that the Professor of Engineering came to putting forward a theory to account for the astonishing facts he had uncovered. It is not a very satisfactory theory. Eclipses of the sun and moon provide far less impressive spectacles in Britain than in most other parts of the inhabited world, and Thom offers no suggestions to explain why the inhabitants of this country should have brought a more scientific attitude to their investigation than more advanced people in sunnier climates to the south, nor why they should have thought it expedient to undertake immense physical and intellectual exertions in order, apparently, to satisfy an idle curiosity. We must not forget D. H. Sadler's point, that the builders of an astronomical observatory designed for the prediction of eclipses must have known the causes of eclipses before they started to build. The questions to be answered are: how did they discover those causes, and why was it so tremendously important for them to know when the next eclipse was going to occur.

Thom's reference to 'Megalithic man' is interesting. As a former Oxford professor he evidently accepted, as was proper, the view of his archaeological colleagues regarding the primitive culture of the men who built the megalithic structures; but it is equally evident that he could not inwardly reconcile that view with the astonishing feats of observation and scientific reasoning that his own calculations showed they must have performed.

To escape from the toils of this conflict he therefore invented this new anthropological phenomenon called 'Megalithic man' — an indigenous British species who differs from all other species of primitive man in that he is not frightened when the sun goes dark or the moon goes blood-red; nor does he invoke his gods or attribute these alarming phenomena to supernatural causes, but jumps to the conclusion that their cause is to be found in the occasional co-incidence of the sun, the moon, and the earth in line with one another. He then measures the period of revolution of the lunar nodes; he observes the almost imperceptible wobble in the moon's orbit; he sets up gigantic stones to mark the extreme positions of the sun and moon to facilitate his observations and help him to calculate the occurrence of the next eclipse; and he does all this without written records or any of the implements that people now need for drawing geometrical figures and doing complex calculations and for educating their children in the elements of mathematics.

A large number of the sites surveyed by Professor Thom were in Scotland, some of the most remarkable being as far away as the Outer Hebrides. It seems that in his vision of 'Megalithic man' the professor conjured up a sort of ideal prototype of his own race, endowed in an extreme degree with the Scot's well-known capacity for giving himself an advanced education without possessing any of the means that are normally required for that purpose by less determined and resourceful people.

However, there was one vital tool that Thom found by these

same surveys that 'Megalithic man' did possess, namely a standard unit of length. This is a tool so important that by itself it practically refutes the conventional archaeological theory and proves that the megalithic builders were civilized men; for the possession of a standard unit of length and its offspring, the standard unit of weight, are the very touchstones of civilization, the keys that open the door to the development of the fundamental arts on which civilizations are built, namely land survey, architecture, engineering, and regulated commerce. [9]

Notes on Chapter 8

1) Souvenir Press, London, 1965.

2) *Nature*, Vol. 210 p. 1302 (1966).

3) *Antiquity*, Vol. XL p. 215 (1966).

4) *Nature*, Vol. 211, p. 454 (1966).

5) *Antiquity*, Vol. XL, p. 271 (1966).

6) *Antiquity*, Vol. XLI No. 163, p. 174 (1967).

7) A. Thom, *Megalithic Sites in Britain* (Oxford University Press, London, 1967).

8) Ibid. p. 23. In the passage quoted above (pages 94-95), Diodorus of Sicily said: 'They say also that the moon, as viewed from this island, appears to be but a little distance from the earth, and to have upon it prominences, like those of the earth, which are visible to the eye'. This sounds very much like an attempt by a non-scientist to report a description, given long ago by astronomers and never since understood, of the way in which not the moon itself but the *motions* of the moon could be measured more nearly in Britain than in Greece, and how such measurements revealed irregularities that were imperceptible at lower latitudes.

9) This chapter was written before the appearance of Professor Thom's second book *Megalithic Lunar Observatories* (O.U.P., 1971). In that work Thom followed up the results of his earlier work by describing in detail a number of megalithic sites that were manifestly laid out as observatories for observing minutely the oscillations of the moon's orbit. The book discusses the possible methods by which the correct alignments for the stones were found. The conclusions show that some of those methods must have been exceedingly complex, and that the mathematical ability of the designers of some of the sites was of a more advanced nature than even Thom himself had previously supposed. He was at last forced to give up all attempts to fit the picture of 'Megalithic man' that emerged spontaneously from his meticulous

surveys into the frame established by the archaeologists. 'As the investigation advanced', he wrote in his Preface, 'it became evident that I was not dealing with monuments orientated for some ritualistic purpose but rather with the remnants of a scientific study of the Moon's motion. When this is recognized it will be found that a great mass of material falls into place. We must no longer assert that these people could not possibly have known this or done that. It has proved much more fruitful to ask ourselves how a *trained scientific mind*' (our italics) 'would have approached their problems, always bearing in mind the kind of facilities which were available.'

The editor of *Antiquity* admitted, after favourable reviews first by an archaeologist and then by an astronomer, that Thom's conclusions must be taken very seriously. The only point on which the second of these reviews (by Douglas C. Heggie of the Institute of Theoretical Astronomy, Cambridge, in *Antiquity*, March 1972) seriously challenged those conclusions was on the question of feasibility. He pointed out that, having regard to the complexities of the moon's motion and the probable amount of interference with observations that would have been caused by the weather, it would have taken 70 years or more of observations before some of the sight lines could have been accurately established; and he suggested that this might 'compel us to search for some alternative explanation of the apparent high accuracy of some of the sites.'

Seventy years may seem like an eternity in the 20th century, but to 'Megalithic man' with his distant view of the universe it was surely more 'like an evening gone'. There is evidence, as we have seen, indicating that the builders of Stonehenge spent a hundred years observing the risings of the full moon nearest the winter solstice, planting stakes to mark the various maxima, before they took the irrevocable step of setting up one of their gigantic stones to mark the exact point of the extreme limit of the moon's travel. Those stones were intended to endure, like the Pyramid, at least for several thousand years if not for ever. A century or so spent in determining their exact location was a tiny fraction of their intended life-span.

9 Arithmetic and Geometry

PROFESSOR THOM'S *Megalithic Sites in Britain* is a landmark in the history of the study of the megalithic culture. It summarises the results of the first systematic attempt ever made to read the message of the Great Stones not by digging round them and under them but by making detailed and accurate surveys of their positions and by subjecting the data so obtained from hundreds of different sites to modern methods of statistical analysis. The conclusions that are important for our purpose may be listed under five headings as they relate respectively to the shapes of the stone circles, the unit of measurement used in their construction, the preferences for certain numbers or groups of numbers, the orientation of the sites, and the accuracy with which the stones were positioned and aligned.

1) *Shape.* With some exceptions the so-called 'stone circles' were not circles at all but complex geometrical figures resembling circles. Some were circles flattened on one side, others elongated or egg-shaped, and others ellipses. In all cases there was evidence that they had been laid out with great precision according to cleverly contrived geometrical constructions. Details of some of these constructions, reproduced from Professor Thom's book, are given in Appendix 1.

2) *Unit of Measurement.* At all the sites surveyed the builders used the same unit of measurement which Thom called the 'megalithic yard' (MY). He established its length as 2.720 feet (32.64 inches) or 829 millimetres. Moreover, since he failed to detect any difference between the values determined from different sites all over Britain, from the south of England (and later, Brittany) to the north of Scotland, he concluded that there must have been a headquarters from which standard rods were sent out, because if each small community had obtained its measure by copying the rod of its neighbour the accumulated error would certainly have exceeded 0.03 inches, and an error of this magnitude would have been easily detected in the statistical analysis.

123

3) *Preferences in numbers.* The builders seem to have had an obsession for whole numbers and abhorred incommensurables. The principal object of the designers in flattening or elongating their circles appears to have been to make the circumferences as well as the radii measurable in whole numbers of megalithic yards. The numbers used are not randomly spread, but a strong preference is shown for the number 5 and its multiples.

In the egg-shaped circles the circumference is made up of arcs of circles drawn from multiple centres which form the points of Pythagorean triangles, i.e. right-angled triangles having whole-number sides. The commonest such triangle is the simplest one with sides 3, 4, 5 units long ($3^2 + 4^2 = 5^2$),[1] but the megalithic builders used others also. Thom was puzzled by the fact that the one he found used next most often was not the next in ascending order of size but the sixth, namely the triangle with sides 12, 35, 37 units long. This is the one that was used at Woodhenge.

4) *Orientation.* From the analysis of his surveys at other megalithic sites Thom found, as Hawkins claimed to have found at Stonehenge, that in a number of cases far too great to be accidental the sightlines formed by using one stone as a backsight and for a foresight either another stone or some distinctive feature on the horizon such as a mountain peak or a 'notch' in the skyline were directed to points where the sun or the moon or a star of the first magnitude would rise or set at critical moments of its path. The axes of the 'circles' were similarly aligned. The histogram of the lunar alignments he plotted showed

> 'a double peak corresponding to the two limbs of the moon. This result was unexpected and it was so unlikely to have happened by accident that it seemed desirable to look more closely into a number of sites where the indication of the necessary azimuth at the site itself was weak. This study showed up that Megalithic man was well acquainted with the small amplitude ripple on the moon's declination and has left such definite indicators that we can, with their help alone, determine its magnitude ... We do not know of any technique which could have been used to examine this oscillation with the moon at the nodes, but they could have made a measurement of its period and may have connected it with the eclipse year'.[2]

5) *Accuracy.* Whenever Thom was able to establish the original direction of these alignments with precision he found that they showed the stones to have been set up with a remarkable degree of accuracy. At Callanish on the island of Lewis in the Outer Hebrides, there is a group of circles in which several astronomical alignments were found to be accurate to within one tenth of one degree. In the measurement of distances he found that at some sites, notably at Avebury, the accuracy with which the stones had been set up approached 1 in 1,000. 'Only an experienced surveyor', he says, '*with good equipment* is likely to attain this kind of accuracy' (our italics).

Let us now consider the value of these five characteristics of the megalithic culture as indicators of its Egyptian origin.

Take the last two points first — orientation and accuracy. The Great Pyramid is oriented to the four cardinal points of the compass with a maximum error of only one twelfth of a degree, and its massive casing stones were cut and positioned so accurately that the average gap between them was about one fiftieth of an inch. This immediately establishes as it were a bond of sympathy between the builders of the Pyramid and the erectors of the megaliths. Nothing approaching such accuracy in the measurement of lengths and angles is found anywhere in the world at this time outside Britain and Egypt.

Consider now the use of numbers. Here we must introduce the reader to the number known as *phi* (ϕ), a unique number which is connected in some profound and mysterious way with the evolution of life.

Phi is an irrational number having the value

$$\phi = \frac{\sqrt{5}+1}{2} = 1.61803...$$

It is the limiting value of the ratio between successive numbers in the Fibonacci series. This is the series of numbers beginning 0, 1, 1, 2, 3, 5, 8, 13 . . . in which each term is the sum of the two previous terms. As the numbers in the series get progressively bigger, so the ratio between each term and its immediate predecessor approximates ever more closely to *phi.*

Phi is unique in that it is the only number whose square is equal to itself plus one and whose reciprocal is equal to itself minus one, thus:

$$\phi + 1 = \phi^2 \text{ ; and } \phi - 1 = \frac{1}{\phi}$$

125

and it is the only irrational number that approaches more closely to rationality the higher the power to which it is raised.

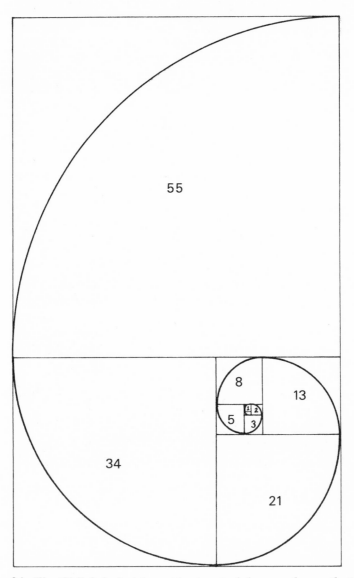

24. The 'Phi' Spiral. *A logarithmic spiral, known also as the 'whirling squares'.*

25. A Sea-Shell. *Radiograph of the shell of the chambered nautilus* (Nautilus pompilius).

In geometry, *phi* appears in pentagonal forms of symmetry, notably in the five-pointed star which was the emblem of the Pythagorean brotherhoods. In biology, there are many plants, molluscs and other living organisms that manifest an extraordinary and so far unexplained predilection either for numbers of the Fibonacci series, or for pentagonal arrangements of petals and other parts, or for logarithmic spirals (notably in sea shells) which expand in the ratio ϕ : 1 with every quarter or half turn. No modern scientist has been able to explain, for example, why the florets in the head of a sunflower always appear at the points of intersection of two sets of logarithmic spirals curving outwards from the centre, one clockwise and the other counter-clockwise, and why the numbers of spirals in the two sets are never equal but are always consecutive numbers in the Fibonacci series, like 21 and 34, or 55 and 89.

In art, the *phi-ratio* was known to the Greeks and Romans, and was used by the architect of the Parthenon to give that temple to the goddess of wisdom its classic beauty. Later, it was studied by some of the great masters of Renaissance painting such as Leonardo da Vinci and Raphael, and by many later artists and designers down to Le Corbusier in modern architecture. Such was the value that these masters placed on its aesthetic merits that they called it the *Golden Section* or the *Divine Proportion*. [3]

No written records have been found on papyri or in inscriptions in tombs or elsewhere to prove that the Egyptians knew anything about the *phi-ratio*, but there is strong circumstantial evidence in their art and architecture that they knew both how to construct it geometrically from a 2 x 1 rectangle and how to derive it arithmetically from numbers in the Fibonacci series. The importance that Egyptian artists attached to it in painting and sculpture was brought to light not long ago by a Norwegian artist, Else Christie Kielland, who set out to discover what were the rules — obviously strict ones — by which the formalised art of ancient Egypt was governed. After studying a great many statues, reliefs and paintings of the Old and the New Kingdoms, the artist found that the factor that most commonly governed their composition was a geometrical construction for the derivation of ϕ. The framework of this construction is a 2 x 1 rectangle and its $\sqrt{5}$ diagonal. It is explained in detail in Appendix 2 together with the way in which Miss Kielland deduced that it was applied to a typical example of Egyptian art dated 2750 BC. A somewhat different construction, she discovered, was used in the designs on the Pallette of Narmer (c. 3200 BC), but the same principle was applied. 'Investigations into the proportions of the Pallette and its division into fields of various sizes show an absolute dependence on the ϕ constructions.' [4]

The use of ϕ in Egyptian architecture has also been studied recently in America, where attention has been drawn to the fact that Egyptian architectural design was largely based on the use of the 5:8 isosceles triangle (named by Viollet-le-Duc 'the Egyptian triangle') in which the height is to the base as 5 is to 8.[5] (This triangle can also be used to construct a regular heptagon, or to divide a circle into 7 equal parts, with a high degree of accuracy — a fact of which the importance will appear later when we discuss the manner in which the circle of 56 Aubrey holes was laid out at Stonehenge.) The Pyramid of Mycerinus, the smallest of the three great pyramids of Gizeh, is based on this triangle. 5 and 8 are consecutive numbers of the Fibonacci series, and $8/5$ (= 1.6)is a fair approximation to ϕ (= 1.618 ..).

A much closer approximation to the *phi-ratio* was obtained by the architects of the Great Pyramid when they used the higher Fibonacci numbers 55 and 89 to determine its half-base and its slope height respectively ($89/55$ = 1.61818). Using a unit of measurement, or modulus, of 4 Royal cubits (= 6 ft. 10.48 ins. or 2.096 m.), they made the base of the Pyramid 110 units square, its height 70 and its slope height or apothem 89 units. The centre elevation is thus very nearly, but not quite, a double Pythagorean triangle, because $55^2 + 70^2 = 7925$, whilst $89^2 = 7921$.

The use of Pythagorean triangles by the megalith builders has already been mentioned. Their use of Fibonacci numbers higher than 5 is not so obvious, but their curious liking for triangles with sides 12, 35, 37 in the egg-shaped circles may be significant in this connection. In the equation of squares we have $144 + 1225 = 1369$. The first of these numbers, 144 (= $55 + 89$) is a Fibonacci number, while the other two are related to one another in the ratio $2 : \sqrt{5}$. They can be nearly derived from the Fibonacci sequence 377, 610, 987, as follows: $377 + 987 = 1364$ (= 1369 —5); $610 \times 2 = 1220$ (= 1225 —5).

More remarkable and, we believe, of more profound significance is the appearance in the Great Pyramid and in the stone circles respectively of two different numerical relations between the irrational numbers ϕ and π (*pi*).

The Great Pyramid triangle in which the hypotenuse (slope height) is ϕ times the length of the short side (half-base) possesses the unique property that the longer of the two sides enclosing the right angle (i.e. the vertical height) is the geometric mean of the other two sides. In trigonometrical terms, it is the only triangle whose sine is equal to its cotangent.

Putting

s = slope height (or apothem)
v = vertical height
b = half base

in the Pyramid triangle, we have the following approximate equations: $s/b = 89/55 = \phi$, and

$$s/v = 89/70 = v/b = 70/55 = \sqrt{\phi} = \phi^{1/2}$$

Now $70/55 = 7/22 \times 4$, so if we put $22/7 = \pi$ we get the equation $4/\pi = \phi^{1/2}$, or

$$\tfrac{1}{4}\pi = \phi^{-1/2} \dots\dots\dots\dots\dots\dots\dots\dots\dots\dots\dots (1)$$

In the two types of flattened stone circle whose geometry is described in Appendix 1 it will be seen that the two equations given by Professor Thom for calculating the lengths of the circumferences both contain the expression $5\pi/6$. Taking π once more as equal to $22/7$, we get $5\pi/6 = 55/21$. Both 55 and 21 are Fibonacci numbers (the sequence is . . . 8, 13, 21, 34, 55 . . .) so, taking $55/34$ and $34/21$ as both equal to ϕ, we have

$$\tfrac{5}{6}\pi = \phi^2 \dots\dots\dots\dots\dots\dots\dots\dots\dots\dots\dots\dots\dots\dots\dots (2)$$

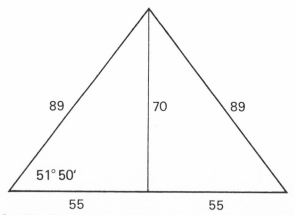

26. The Proportions of the Great Pyramid. *The dimensions shown are in units of 4 Royal cubits. The sides of the right-angled triangles are in the proportion $\emptyset : \sqrt{\emptyset} : 1$.*

The actual numerical values of the terms on either side of equation (1) are 0.78540 and 0.78615 respectively — a coincidence exact to within an accuracy better than 1 in 1000. The coincidence of the terms of equation (2) is even closer, the values being respectively 2.61799 and 2.61803 — a difference of 1 in 85,000. This equation is well known to arithmeticians as one of the most extraordinary coincidences in mathematics.

It is extremely unlikely that either equation occurs in its architectural context by accident. In the case of the Pyramid the entire structure of that vast edifice depends on the choice of the geometric series 55:70:89. These numbers must have been chosen with the utmost care. It is inconceivable that the fact that both the first and the last of them are Fibonacci numbers could be fortuitous having regard to the appearance of the *phi-ratio* elsewhere in Egyptian art and architecture. The appearance of the *pi-ratio* is even more clearly manifest in the design because the ratio of the base perimeter (8 times the half-base, or 440 units of 4 Royal cubits) to the vertical height is 2π, which means that its length is equal to that of the circumference of a circle whose radius is the vertical height of the Pyramid. For a long time it was thought that this feature — the 'squaring of the circle' — was the *only* mathematical relation that governed the architectural design.

In the stone circles we might be inclined to regard the appearance of $5\pi/6$ as no more than a remarkable coincidence if it occurred in the geometrical construction of only one type of circle, or if it resulted from the employment of the same geometric principle in both types. But in 'Type A' circles (see Appendix 1) the fraction 5/6 is arrived at, in effect, by adding 1/6 to 2/3 and in 'Type B' circles by adding 1/3 to 1/2. The two constructions are probably the only ones it is possible to devise which embody $5\pi/6$ and which also make the circumference of the circle approximately equal to integral 3 times the length of the long diameter. Both constructions are of the utmost elegance. One produces a circumference 3.0591 times, the other 2.9572 times the diameter. The mean of these numbers is 3.0081. It looks as if the builders followed the precedent set by their mathematical god in the Fibonacci series itself, where the ratios between successive pairs of numbers alternately just exceed and just fall short of ϕ, and that they decided to build their flattened circles alternately first of one type and then of the other in order to get the *average* ratio as close as possible to integral 3.

If we are right in supposing that our two *pi/phi* equations were incorporated of set purpose, one in the Pyramid and the other in the stone circles of the megalith builders, the question arises: what meaning must be attached to these curious number relations? They must, surely, have conveyed some message to

131

those who could understand it. What kind of a message could it possibly have been?

We shall suggest a possible answer to this riddle in our story at the end of the book, and a clue to it is included later in the present chapter. But first it is necessary to consider what is perhaps the most striking connection of all between the Great Pyramid and the stone circles. This is to be found in the units of measurement used in their constructions.

The unit used by the builders of the Pyramid was the Royal cubit (Rc) of 20.62 ins. (524 mm.). This was $\sqrt{2}$ Egyptian remens of 14.58 ins. (370 mm.), or the length of the diagonal of a 1 x 1 remen square. The practical use of this curious $\sqrt{2}$: 1 ratio is probably to be found in land measurement: a square field of side n Rc would be exactly double the area of one of side n remens, and half one of side $2n$ remens or n double remens. By using these two different units of measurement the Egyptians were thus able to avoid getting themselves tied up in very difficult calculations involving the irrational number $\sqrt{2}$ whenever they wanted to double or halve land areas.

Professor Thom deduced from his surveys that the builders of the stone circles used a 'Megalithic Yard' (MY) of 32.64 ins. (892 mm.). The ratio MY : Rc is $\sqrt{5}$: $\sqrt{2}$ to the nearest millimetre, which makes the MY equal to $\sqrt{5}$ remens, or the length of the diagonal of a 2 x 1 remen rectangle.

We have already seen that the 2 x 1 rectangle and its $\sqrt{5}$ diagonal were invested with deep religious significance for Egyptian artists due to their being the point of departure for the geometrical construction of the *phi-ratio* $(\sqrt{5} + 1)/2$ (see Appendix 2). There are also grounds for believing that $\sqrt{5}$ and its powers 5 and 25 were sacred numbers in themselves. In Egyptian number mysticism 3 was the number that represented mind or spirit, personified as Osiris; 4 stood for earth or body, personified as Isis; and 5 symbolised life, the compound of mind and body, or Horus, the offspring of Osiris and Isis. The Pythagorean 3, 4, 5 triangle was sacred because it thus represents the Holy Trinity of the Osirian religion: mind and body in dimensions at right angles to one another, joined together to produce life, the hypotenuse that runs transversely across both.

This symbolism is enshrined mysteriously in the construction of the Pyramid. In the secret passages and chambers in its interior we find the $\sqrt{5}$ diagonal of the 2 x 1 rectangle used in the vertical plane. The Ascending and Descending Corridors and the

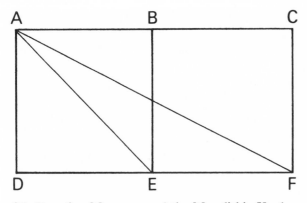

27. Egyptian Measures and the Megalithic Yard

AB = AD = BC = 1 Remen = 14.58 ins. = 370 mm.
AE = 1 Royal cubit (Rc) = 20.62 ins. = 524 mm.
AF = 1 Megalithic Yard (MY) = 32.64 ins. = 829 mm.
1 Rc = √2 Remen; 1 MY = √5 Remen.
500 Remens = 600 Greek feet = 1 Olympic Stade.
10 Olympic Stades = 6075 ft. = 1 nautical mile (app.) = 1852 m.
216,000 (= 60^3) Olympic Stades = the Earth's circumference.

Grand Gallery slope at a gradient of 1 in 2 and thus form the diagonals of such rectangles.[6] In the so-called King's Chamber, the Holy of Holies situated in the centre of the Pyramid, the architect used a modulus of 5 Rc as the unit of measurement, in contrast to the 4 Rc used in the external dimensions. This accords with the number symbolism whereby 4 represents the body (the external casing) and 5 the life within.

The plan of the King's Chamber is a 2 x 1 rectangle. The floor measures 4 x 2 units of 5 Rc, and thus has a diagonal of 2√5. The mean height of the Chamber (symbolically its most significant dimension) as measured by Sir Flinders Petrie, is about 19 ft. 3 ins. (5.85 m.) which is within half an inch of 5√5 Rc or √5 units. The end walls are thus 2 x √5 rectangles and their diagonals are exactly 3 units.

The length of the chamber being 4 and the diagonal of the end walls 3, the grand diagonal from one corner of the floor to the opposite corner of the ceiling is therefore 5. It is thus apparent that the whole Chamber was designed to enshrine the sacred 3, 4, 5 triangles which fit transversely down its length between floor and ceiling, cutting through all the 3 dimensions of the Chamber.

133

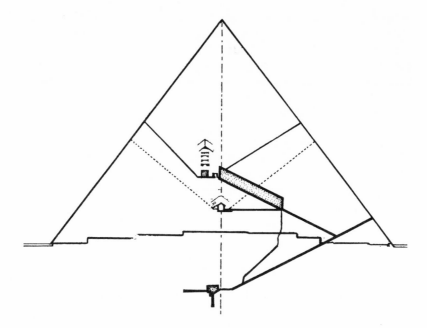

28. Section through the Great Pyramid

It is generally supposed that the King's Chamber was the place where the Pharaoh's body was buried with its accompanying treasures, and that the Chamber was entered by tomb robbers in antiquity and denuded of all its contents, all that was left being an empty sarcophagus. But there is no evidence to indicate, let alone prove, that this is what happened. We think it more likely that the king's body was buried in the customary place, namely in the underground tomb hewn out of the rock beneath the Pyramid (where robbers would be more likely to find it), and that the chambers and corridors in the interior were built solely for reasons of religious symbolism. On this interpretation the sarcophagus was never intended to be occupied but was put empty into the otherwise bare King's Chamber to symbolise the resurrection of the body or the continuance of life after death through reincarnation.[7]

We come lastly to the shape of the stone rings. Can we discern here any points of resemblance that might link them with the Nile culture?

At first sight, No. There is no architectural monument in Egypt even remotely resembling any of the megalithic structures.

Indeed, the stone ring might be considered the exact antithesis of the characteristic Egyptian monument, the pyramid. But that in itself may be significant. In our story we shall use it as a clue to a possible interpretation of a symbolic relation between the two types of structure.

There is, however, one feature that suggests more directly a consanguinity of ideas. This is to be found in the egg-shaped rings. We have already seen that these are complex geometrical

29. Egg-Shaped Stone Ring, Allan Water, Roxburghshire. *From the survey drawing by Prof. A. Thom.*

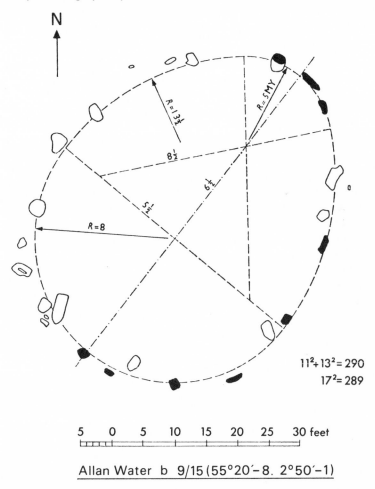

$$11^2 + 13^2 = 290$$
$$17^2 = 289$$

5   0   5   10   15   20   25   30 feet

Allan Water b 9/15 (55°20′- 8. 2°50′-1)

135

constructions based on Pythagorean triangles, with a preference for the sacred 3, 4, 5 triangle of the Osirian Trinity. We now observe that the egg shape itself has meaning in Egyptian religion, as symbolic of the cycle of birth, death, and rebirth.

The egg is used nowadays all over the world as a symbol of resurrection from death, but the idea is much older than Christianity and may well have originated in megalithic times. The egg symbol is, in fact, more appropriate to the Eastern belief in reincarnation than it is to Christian beliefs, because Christ's resurrection did not involve a physical act of rebirth. The practice of giving eggs at Easter was a pagan practice which was adapted, like many other such practices, by the early Christians. They painted their eggs red to represent the blood of Christ, or marked them with spots of different colours in memory of the tears of the Blessed Virgin Mary.

In the ancient Egyptian myth, Ra the Sun god himself was born anew every morning from an egg.[8]

Notes on Chapter 9

1) In 1970 Thom surveyed an unusual site in Brittany, dated circa 2000 BC, called the 'Cromlech de Crucuno'. The stones at this site are arranged in a rectangle, the sides of which measure exactly 30 x 40 MY and the diagonals 50 MY.

2) A. Thom, *Megalithic Sites in Britain*, p. 165.

3) For a full account of the history of the application of *phi* in Western art and architecture see Matila C. Ghyka, *Le Nombre d'Or: Rites et Rythmes Pythagoriciens dans le Développement de la Civilisation Occidentale* (Gallimard, Paris, 1931). For details of *phi's* mathematical and aesthetic properties see H. E. Huntley, *The Divine Proportion, A Study in Mathematical Beauty* (Dover Publications Inc., New York, 1970).

4) Else Christie Kielland, *Geometry in Egyptian Art* (Alec Tiranti Ltd., London, 1955, p. 99).

5) A. Badawy, *Ancient Egyptian Architectural Design: A Study of the Harmonic System*. (University of California Publications, Near Eastern Studies, 1965, Vol. 4.).

6) The angle of which the tangent is exactly ½ is 26° 34′ to the nearest minute. The angle of the Descending Passage, as measured by Piazzi Smyth and later by Sir Flinders Petrie, is 26° 17′. Petrie found that the mean variation from a central axis along the entire length of 350 feet was less than ¼ inch in azimuth and only 1/10th inch in

altitude. Men who could tunnel a hole into solid rock with such astounding accuracy would be unlikely to make an error of 17 minutes of arc in its angle of slope, which amounts to 1 per cent in the horizontal component. A possible reason for the choice of 26° 17′, suggested by R. A. Proctor in 1883, is that that angle lined up with what was then the Pole Star, i.e. the star by which the position of the celestial North Pole could be most easily identified, at the lower culmination of its nightly journey round the Pole. This theory was put forward in the light of a remark by the Neoplatonist philosopher Proclus in his commentary on Plato's *Timaeus* to the effect that the Pyramid was used as an astronomical observatory before its completion. See Peter Tompkins, *Secrets of the Great Pyramid* (Weidenfeld, London 1972). Even if this theory is right, it would not follow that the Egyptian astronomers saw no mystical significance in the extraordinary closeness of the approach of the astral alignment to a perfect √5 slope, or that they did not choose the star that gave the nearest approach to that slope in preference to the brightest star near the Pole. Indeed, there is reason to suppose that this is just what they did, because during the most likely period of the Pyramid's construction (c. 2500 BC) the then Pole Star (Thuban, or Alpha Draconis) was too near the Pole to give the required altitude.

7) M. André Pochan has put forward an interesting theory of the religious symbolism of the chambers in the Great Pyramid. He believes they were used for Isiac rites in which the divine spirit of the dead Pharaoh was resurrected in the person of the new Pharaoh his successor, and that the empty sarcophagus played an essential part in this ritual. He argues that all 3 burial chambers were used for different stages of the ritual, and that the true burial place is a tomb 58 metres below ground, which has never been discovered. See André Pochan, *L'Enigme de la Grand Pyramide* (Robert Laffont, Paris, 1971).

8) On the meaning of numbers and geometric proportions generally in Egyptian religious art, and the *phi-ratio* in particular, see R. A. Schwaller de Lubicz, *Le Temple dans l'Homme* (Imprimerie Schindler, Cairo 1949). '*Le Nombre d'Or ne joue pas seulement comme fonction d'une proportion idéale, mais sert de base à une philosophie faisant la relation entre l'état métaphysique et l'état physique. C'est en cela que consiste son caractère sacré.*' The author of this profound observation was a French philosopher and orientalist who spent twelve years surveying and studying the tombs and temples at Luxor and their inscriptions. The deep insight he thus acquired into the ancient Egyptian way of thought enabled him to interpret many signs and symbols whose meanings have been missed by professional Egyptologists of the conventional school. 'Schwaller's interpretaion (of the architecture of the Temple of Luxor) not only overthrows everything orthodox Egyptologists believe, but, if he is correct, then modern man's cherished belief in "progress" is a fiction . . . "The Temple" was a

society more or less secret (or at any rate secretive) which passed on to its members the esoteric keys to universal knowledge, and which, behind the scenes, directed the art and architecture of the country . . . Most religious traditions insist that at one time science, art, religion, and philosophy were complementary and interdependent — not mutually exclusive as they are today. Schwaller maintains that Egypt was such a civilization, and that its comprehensive knowledge of cosmic laws are embodied in its art and architecture; a permanent secret to those unaware or immune to such knowledge, but a permanent source of instruction to those in possession of the key.' J. A. West, *A New Look at Ancient Egypt* (Man, Myth & Magic, Purnell, Part 95).

Unlike Hawkins' book on Stonehenge, Schwaller de Lubicz' book on the Temple of Luxor with its new interpretation of the geometry of that extraordinary building was not challenged by the archaeologists. Instead they ignored it, just as they have ignored, or dismissed without scientific examination of the evidence, claims by others to have discovered hidden mathematical, astronomical, or philosophical meanings in the geometry of the Great Pyramid.

10 The Aubrey Holes

THE AUBREY HOLES at Stonehenge are described by Professor Atkinson as 'roughly circular pits, varying in width from 30 to 70 ins. (75 to 180 cm.), and from 24 to 45 ins. (60 to 115 cm.) in depth. The sides are steep and the bottoms flat'. They are set in what appears to be an accurate circle just inside the bank and ditch that surrounds the whole enclosure, and they are regularly spaced at an average distance of 16 ft. (4.9m.) from one another round the circumference. The diameter of the circle given by Professor Atkinson was 288 ft. (88 m.) and its centre was located by him at a point about 3 ft. (1 m.) SSW of the centre of the sarsen circle; but measurements made recently by the Department of the Environment on the master copy of their survey drawing gave the mean *radius* as 140 ft. 4 ins. $\pm$ 1 ft. 10 ins. $(42.77 \pm 0.56$ m.). The radius cannot be determined precisely because the ring is not a true circle and it is impossible to find a centre from which to draw one circle that cuts through all the holes (only 34 of which have actually been excavated).

From the holes themselves no clue can be obtained as to the purpose for which they were made beyond the fact that they were evidently not intended to receive megaliths. Those that have been excavated have been found to be filled with the chalk rubble that was originally dug out of them and then 'apparently shovelled back soon afterwards, some of it having been burnt meanwhile.' In most of the holes there were deposits of cremated human bones, but the date when these burials took place is not known. According to Professor Atkinson the holes were dug before even the bluestones were erected, at the same time as the bank and ditch, when perhaps the only stone at Stonehenge was the Heel Stone and the rest of the structure was of timber.

We have already referred to Professor Hawkins' theory that the holes were dug to contain movable markers to mark the place of the current year in the cycle of eclipses. This theory has been rejected on both astronomical and archaeological grounds. Professor Hoyle's related theory that the Aubrey circle

139

constituted a protractor representing the circle of the ecliptic round which markers were moved to simulate the motions of the sun, the moon, and the lunar nodes, fails on the same archaeological grounds. But the idea that the circle was a protractor may provide a clue to a different solution of the problem.

If the object of the builders of Stonehenge was to make accurate observations of celestial bodies they would need some means of measuring the azimuth (i.e. the direction in the horizontal plane) of those bodies at their risings and settings, and the simplest way to do this would be to measure their position on the circumference of a circle relative to fixed marks on a graduated scale. To obtain an accuracy of, say one twelfth of a degree (5 minutes of arc) the circle would need to be divided into $360 \times 12 = 4320$ parts; and to be visible from the centre, the scale of the 'protractor' would need to be set up on posts all round the circumference.

It would be both uneconomical and, in a barbarian country, unsafe to construct a permanent scale of four thousand marks on an elevated structure round the perimeter of the site. The sensible thing to do would be to establish the positions of, say, 60 primary points at intervals of 6 degrees by digging holes in the ground, and, for fine readings, to rely on a movable apparatus consisting of two upright posts joined together by a horizontal beam on which would be carved the graduated scale of 72 subdivisions. The apparatus would be set up in two adjacent holes on that part of the circle where it was desired to make the next observations. When no observations were in progress it would be removed to a safe place under cover, leaving nothing on the perimeter of the circle for vandals to destroy. The holes would be lined with timber for accuracy and kept filled with rubble when not in use.

To measure the azimuth of a point on the horizon by reference to such a scale it would be necessary for the observer to stand some distance behind the centre of the circle and for the centre point to be marked with a pointed marker to act as backsight for his sight-line to the object. Excavations at Stonehenge have shown that the earliest stone structure inside the bank and ditch consisted of a double ring of bluestones set, apparently, in a complete circle concentric with the ring of Aubrey Holes. The mean diameters of the two rings are given by Professor Atkinson as 74 and 86 feet (22.6 and 26.2m.) respectively. The stones were arranged in pairs, each stone of the outer ring being placed outside one on the inner ring and on the same radius from the centre. Our suggestion is that these stones (replacing an earlier wooden structure) were set up to support an elevated walkway some 6 feet (2 m.) wide on which an observer would stand to observe the risings and settings of sun, moon, and stars across a backsight in the centre of the circle and through a foresight on the scale on the far side. This would give him the necessary height to see over bushes and perhaps roofs of low buildings, and the horizontal beam of the scale would be used as an artificial horizon to eliminate inaccuracies caused by irregularities in the ground horizon.

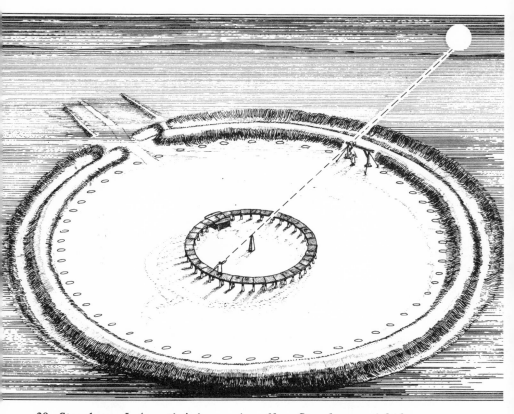

30. Stonehenge I. *An artist's impression of how Stonehenge might have looked before the erection of any of the megaliths. An observer on the viewing platform is measuring the azimuth of the rising moon.*

141

The backsight would have consisted of a pointed obelisk. There is no sign today of any tall stone standing in the centre of the circle, but there is evidence that one bluestone megalith was at one time smashed to smithereens and its fragments systematically scattered all over the site. If an obelisk had been erected there as we suggest, it would have been the most prominent feature of the whole structure. By Christian times it would have been weathered down into the shape of a phallus; and no doubt it would have been regarded by Church and people as a work of Satan erected as an object of worship by heathen devil-worshippers, and meet to be destroyed accordingly.

The exact azimuth of, say, the full-moon-rise would be read off from the scale by means of a pointer attached to the foresight. This would consist of a frame that could be slid along the beam by an assistant acting on signals from the observer. (Figure 31.) Given that the distance of the frame from the observer's eye would be about 180 ft. (55 m.), then, in order to get the moon's disc just framed in the foresight, we estimate that the distance between the uprights of the frame would have to be about 20 to 21 ins. (51 to 53 cm.) apart, or about 1 Egyptian Royal cubit of 20.62 ins. (524 mm.). Another pointer midway between the uprights would help in getting the disc properly centred in the frame, and would be essential for taking readings on a star. (Figure 32.)

31. The Scale. *A subdivision of 1/10th Rc (= 5cm) would subtend an angle of 2 minutes at the centre.*

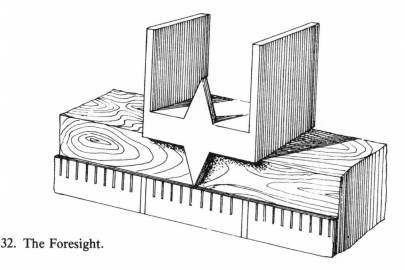

32. The Foresight.

One problem which would be serious when the sun was being observed was that of dazzle. Even at its lowest point on the horizon it is not possible on a clear day to gaze directly at the sun without hurt to the eyes, and the ancients had no dark glass. The archaeological evidence suggests that the problem was solved by lighting fires on the bank behind the scale to produce an opaque screen of smoke. This would account for the bits of burnt chalk that have been found at the bottom of the Aubrey holes, where it would be used as a filling to level the hole after use. Whenever there was a corpse to be buried the fire would be used as a funeral pyre. Burning flesh makes excellent smoke. After burning, the remains would be swept back into the holes with the chalk rubble or shovelled unceremoniously into the outer ditch.

An apparatus such as we have described could have been used by astronomers for making a catalogue of stars, showing their declinations and the dates of their risings and settings. Such a catalogue might have been ordered by the Chief Astronomer-Priest in Heliopolis. It could have been needed for the making of an accurate calendar and it could have been used also for the siting of the Stonehenge marker stones, and for the orientation of stone circles built elsewhere. Its construction would involve the apparatus having to be moved at intervals from one pair of holes to the next systematically all round the circle. After each move it

143

would be calibrated by reference to a landmark on the horizon or a pointed stake planted in the mound outside the circle; and to keep the posts vertically upright in a high wind it would probably be necessary to stay them with guy-ropes. Such a use of the apparatus would explain the archaeological finding that the holes were filled up again very soon after they were dug. Once the catalogue was complete there would be no further use for them.

A problem to which this theory offers no solution is why, for a protractor of this nature, they dug 56 holes rather than 60 as one would expect, and how they managed to get the holes so evenly spaced. Can we find a clue here in the geometry of the other stone 'circles' that were surveyed by Professor Thom?

Thom noticed that his Megalithic man seemed to have a horror of irrational numbers, especially the number *pi*. He resorted to elaborate geometrical constructions in order to make the perimeters of his rings an integral number of times the length of the radii, and he was fond of using double Pythagorean triangles in some of these constructions. Could it be that the Aubrey circle is not a true circle because it is the result of another of these constructions? Given a pin or a peg and a piece of string, nothing is easier than to fix a number of points accurately on the circumference of a circle; so why, when the builders were so successful in the really difficult task of spacing the 56 holes evenly round the circumference, did they fail to get the radial distances completely accurate?

We have already observed that an isosceles triangle of base 8 and height 5 (the 'Egyptian triangle') could be used to construct a regular heptagon (a 7-sided polygon with all its sides and angles equal) with a high degree of, though not complete, accuracy. Now the division of an arc into 8 equal parts is easily accomplished by 3 successive bisections, but there is no geometrical method of dividing one into 7 equal parts. It therefore seems more likely that the 56 divisions were made by dividing the complete circle by 7 and then each seventh by 8 than the other way round. The 5 : 8 triangle is an obvious starting point for such a procedure. One possible construction based on this principle is set out in Appendix 3.

One piece of evidence that seems to support the idea that the 5 : 8 triangle may have been used in the lay-out of Stonehenge is to be found in the location of the site. The angle of which the cosine is 5/8 (= 0.625) is 51° 19′. The latitude of Stonehenge is 51° 10′.8, of which the cosine is 0.6263. The exact 5/8 line of

144

latitude runs along the Vale of Pewsey about 9 miles to the north, roughly half way between Stonehenge and Avebury. It would be very strange if this siting of the 2 oldest megalithic settlements were just a coincidence. Egyptian astronomers wanting to establish the declinations of celestial bodies would have been

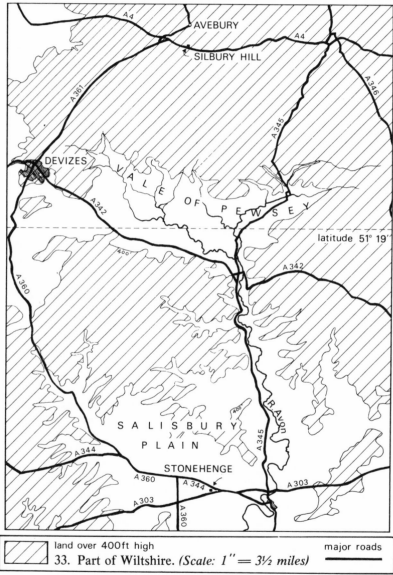

land over 400ft high   major roads

33. Part of Wiltshire. *(Scale: 1" = 3½ miles)*

compelled to site their observatory at a latitude of which the cosine was a simple fraction, because calculations involving division by complicated numbers would have been beyond the capacity of their clumsy system of numerical notation.[2]

Assuming that the Aubrey holes were located as suggested in Appendix 3, the next questions are: what unit of measurement was used, and how was the size of the circle determined?

Stonehenge was not among the megalithic sites that was surveyed by Professor Thom, but he listed it with other circular sites that he had not surveyed in order to check that the diameters as measured by others gave the same results as those of the rings he had measured himself. A statistical analysis of 26 such circles confirmed that the unit of measurement used was the MY of 2.720 feet (829 mm.). The diameter of the Aubrey circle he took from the old Ministry of Public Building and Works survey as 285 ft. (87.0 m.), which is only a little short of 105 MY.[3] Taking π = 22/7, the circumference of a circle of diameter 105 works out at exactly 330.

Remembering the megalithic people's preferences for multiples of 5 and for integral numbers in both diameters and circumferences, these figures provide impressive evidence that the Aubrey circle was laid out in megalithic yards like the other circles, and that its size was chosen in order to satisfy those purely mathematical requirements. But if we take the figures now given by the Department of the Environment (successor to the old Ministry of Public Building and Works), from which the most probable diameter can be taken as something between 277 ft. and 284 ft. 4 ins. (84.4 and 86.5 m.) the fit is not so good.

Consider now the implications of the theory that the circle was laid out as suggested in Appendix 3, and that the men who designed it were priests of the same mathematico-religious order as those who designed the Great Pyramid of Cheops.

For the centre elevation of the Pyramid the designers chose, as we have seen, an arrangement of numbers (110, 70, 89) that gave them the angle of the *phi-ratio* contained in what was very nearly but not quite a double Pythagorean triangle ($55^2 + 70^2$ = 7925; 89^2 = 7921). Their unit measure was the Royal cubit (Rc) of 20.62 ins. (524 mm.), and for the external dimensions of the Pyramid they used a modulus of 4 Rc.

For the 5 : 8 triangle an almost equally good numerical arrangement can be obtained by choosing a base of 40 and a height of 25 units. This makes a nearly perfect double

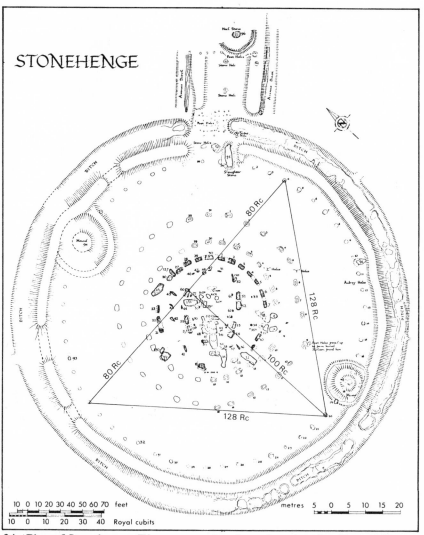

34. Plan of Stonehenge. *The corners of an isosceles triangle of base 160 and height 100 Rc exactly fit over Aubrey holes 4, 20, and 36, pointing due south*

Pythagorean triangle with the sloping sides almost exactly 32 units. $(20^2 + 25^2 = 1025; 32^2 = 1024)$. A circle circumscribing such a triangle would have a diameter of 41 units. If we now divide this number into the diameter of the Aubrey circle as measured by the Department, we get a modulus of 82.15 ± 1.07 ins. $(2.087 \pm 0.027$ m.).

147

The Pyramid modulus of 4 Rc (82.48 ins. or 2.095 m.) falls well within the extreme values thus calculated for the Aubrey circle, and it is less than one centimetre from the mean — a difference of 0.4 per cent. This is much too close a fit to be lightly dismissed as a chance coincidence. The accompanying diagram (Figure 34) shows how the corners of a double Pythagorean triangle of height 100 Rc (= 25 x 4 Rc) and base 160 Rc exactly fit over Aubrey holes 4, 20 and 36, with the apex pointing due south. (This has been checked on the master copy of the survey drawing held by the Department.) The coincidence is much closer than that given by supposing that the diameter of the circle was intended to be 105 MY.

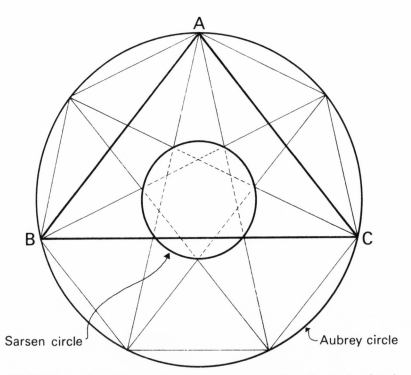

35. 7-Pointed Star. *The circle of sarsen stones at Stonehenge is related to the Aubrey hole circle by this geometrical construction.*

Another curious geometrical feature of the Stonehenge lay-out which was first noticed by Mr. C. A. Newham is illustrated in figure 35: that if you draw a 7-pointed star and fit the points over

7 Aubrey holes in the manner shown, the diameter of a circle circumscribing the smaller heptagon in the centre of the star is exactly equal to that of the sarsen circle measured through the centres of the stones. (All Thom's measurements were made through the centres of stones.)

It may be asked why the megalithic architects should have used two different measures, the Royal cubit at Stonehenge and the Megalithic Yard elsewhere. The answer that suggests itself is that Stonehenge I was the first megalithic structure to be built by the Egyptians in Britain (after their abortive effort in Wales), and it was designed for a purely scientific purpose. The architect therefore used the measure he had been accustomed to using in Egypt. For later circles built for different purposes a new unit was adopted that had a symbolic significance as incorporating the mystic number $\sqrt{5}$.

Both measures show similar derivations from the Egyptian remen. (Figure 27.)

Notes on Chapter 10

1) R. J. C. Atkinson, *Stonehenge* (Hamish Hamilton London , 1956, p. 12).

2) See Chapter 3, p. 49. It may be asked how any people at that time could have established the latitude of a site with such accuracy. The shadow method of measuring the height of the sun at noon is generally supposed to be too imprecise for this purpose because the edge of any shadow cast by an object in sunshine is blurred. However, experiments carried out by Mr Adrian Digby with a metal bar set up to simulate an ancient Mexican trapeze sundial showed that shadow readings of the sun's elevation could be obtained with an accuracy of 2 minutes of arc in the best cases, and a mean of 5 minutes. The outer edge of the penumbra, where the sun's disc begins to be obscured, is blurred, but the edge of the umbra, where the last gleam of light finally disappears, can be finely determined with the aid of a sharp line drawn on the surface onto which the shadow is cast.

3) A. Thom, *Megalithic Sites in Britain*, p. 44.

Part Three The Story

11 The Founding of Stonehenge

IN THE preceding chapters our aim has been to present the facts and figures that seem to us to have a bearing on the origin and history of the megalithic culture and to examine them as a scientist might examine a collection of bones found in a cave with a view to determining what kind of a creature they belonged to.

In this and the following chapters we shall try to put some flesh on these bones. This is a job not for a scientist but for an artist, preferably one who specialises in the imaginative reconstruction of prehistoric scenes. But we ourselves are not specialists. There are, in fact, no specialists in this field; we are all amateurs. Unlike crime fiction, this is a real life detective story in which the reader's guess as to what actually happened is just as likely to be right as the author's; and either guess, provided it fits the facts, is as likely to be right as the theories of scientists who have spent their lives studying this problem. For in all fields of study, be it archaeology or Elizabethan literature or even nuclear physics, the experts who discover the facts cannot claim to possess a monopoly of intelligence when it comes to interpreting them. Indeed, the amateur Holmes is sometimes in a better position to unmask the criminal than the man from the Yard who is officially in charge of the case.

The first thing a detective normally does when faced with an apparently inexplicable crime is to look for a motive. In the Mystery of the Megaliths, an adequate and intelligible motive is conspicuously absent. Why on earth should an isolated community of intelligent people struggling to keep themselves housed and fed decide to devote a huge proportion of its total available resources of time and energy to the task of quarrying and transporting over long distances stones of fantastic size, and erecting them with such uncanny precision that 4000 years later a modern engineer could deduce to the nearest millimetre the length of their unit of measurement, and to a small fraction of a degree the amplitude of the wobble in the moon's orbit of which the very existence was unknown to European astronomers before the 16th century AD?

We accept Professor Thom's conclusion that many of the stone rings and alignments were designed as lunar observatories and used for the prediction of eclipses; but we do not accept his surmise that the ultimate motive of the megalithic builders was nothing more than scientific enquiry. Nor do we accept the view of the archaeologists that the builders were motivated by nothing more than religious fervour. We believe that both science and religion played their part, but the dominant motives that induced so many people to undertake such herculean labours over so long a period were practical and economic.

Our story begins, therefore, with a suggestion as to the motives of the founders of the megalithic culture; and it begins like the story of western civilization itself, in Egypt.

In Egypt the sun shines day after day, year in year out, with deadly monotony, its face only occasionally hidden by cloud, its torrid rays more a burden than a pleasure for the workers toiling in the fields. That the sun will rise and set tomorrow as it rose and set yesterday, travelling from east to west along the same path at the same unalterable speed is as certain as anything can be. Moreover, the heat of the Egyptian sun is lethal. It parches the soil; it is the father not of living things but of the desert.

For the astronomer-priests of Ra, therefore, to have succeeded in persuading the people to worship that pitiless ball of flame as a living and beneficent deity was no insignificant achievement. To peasants and farmers it must have been evident that the source of life was the fertilising waters of the Nile. Those waters impregnated Mother Earth and on them men were dependent for the germination of their crops and the watering of their flocks and herds. Yet Khnum, the ram-headed god of the Nile, though he was revered as the father of all living things, the primordial potter on whose wheel gods and men alike were fashioned, was only a minor deity compared with the great sun god Ra whose temple at Heliopolis outshone all others in magnificence. How was it then that the priests of Ra were able to show that the sun was more worthy of the people's prayers and sacrifices than the river?

There is only one feature in which the sun resembles a sentient and capricious living creature; namely in the fact that at irregular and seemingly unpredictable intervals it hides its face for a while and brings down on the earth in daytime the chill and darkness of night. In northern latitudes a solar eclipse can occur without being noticed, but in the clear air of sun-drenched Egypt the effect of brilliant day turning suddenly into night is terrifying. It was this terror, this sudden fear that it might go out altogether that gave the sun its aspect of divinity in the eyes of the people; and it was on this fear that the priests worked to keep the people in the paths of righteousness and themselves in a state of reasonable affluence.

Ever since the dawn of civilization the cause of eclipses was known to the mathematical élite. But although they knew that eclipses were the effect of the transit of the moon in front of the sun the method they used for predicting them was not scientific. It consisted simply of keeping accurate records and calculating the dates of the recurring *Saros* cycle of eclipses of 18 years and $11\frac{1}{3}$ days in which the pattern repeats itself with only slight variation.

In the weeks preceding a solar eclipse the church of Ra would mount a campaign against the sins and backslidings of the people, calling for more sacrifices and intensification of effort to obey the will of the god. Declaring that Ra was angry with his people, the priests would threaten that he would hide his face from them and desert them altogether unless their conduct improved. When the day came, the High Priest would announce that the god was not satisfied. That day he would leave the world in darkness unless men and women everywhere redoubled their efforts to please him.

As the moon's shadow darkened the earth the terrified people ran to heap their most precious possessions on the altars in a desperate attempt to avert the threatened catastrophe. Then, when the last ounce of sacrificial effort had been wrung from them, the dramatic news would be broken that the supreme Divinity had yielded to the priest's intercession and consented to forgive his sinful subjects; very soon he would shine forth again in all his glory. Great was the people's rejoicing and their gratitude to the priests when the sun shone again.

For centuries these rituals kept the people in constant awe of the sun god's power. They were supplemented by mythical stories that represented Ra as a father figure in human form, and these stories were interwoven with the legends of Osiris and Isis. But solar eclipses remained for the people the only palpable evidence that the priests were in direct communication with the godhead

154

and were able by intercession to turn away his wrath. It would not be putting it too highly to say that the power and wealth of the great church of the sun god in the Old Kingdom was wholly dependent on the ability of its priest-mathematicians to predict eclipses.

Now the 18-year Saros cycle is not exact. At any given point on the earth's surface the pattern of eclipses is repeated more nearly at every third cycle (54 years and 1 month) than in the intervening two, but over a period of about six centuries an eclipse that was total at a certain place at the beginning of the period ceases to be visible at all from that place at the end. It was a matter of great concern to the priests of Ra when they found that their predictions were becoming increasingly erratic with the passage of time.

A diminution of popular faith in the sun god due to this cause as the Old Kingdom passed its zenith coincided with rising resentment against the burden of taxes imposed in the name of religion for the vast works needed to preserve the bodies and souls of the Pharaohs after death. As religious faith weakened and attendances at temple rituals fell off, the astronomer-priests cast about them with growing concern for any means in their power to arrest the trend. After a particularly disastrous year in which there occurred a total eclipse that they had not predicted whereas one whose advent they had loudly proclaimed was scarcely noticeable, the High Priest and Chief Astronomer decided it was necessary to take drastic steps to improve the accuracy of their predictions. He sent accordingly for the most brilliant mathematician in the priesthood and instructed him to study the causes of recent failures and to report on how to improve the standard of eclipse prediction.

The young man reported that the ancient pre-Sumerian records on which they had always relied were now out of date, and that since no suitable records had been kept since the Flood it would be necessary to calculate the dates of future eclipses from current observations. This could be done with the facilities available at the Heliopolis observatory but for one factor. A comparison between calculated and observed phenomena showed that the inclination of the moon's orbit to the ecliptic was not constant, as had been supposed, but was subject to some irregularity which would have to be studied by observation before its effects on eclipses could be precisely predicted. He had been unable to measure this movement in the confined space of the observatory at Heliopolis, but if a new observatory could be set up on an open site with a wide range of vision, preferably at a high latitude, it should be possible to determine the exact nature of the movement from measurements in azimuth of the points of moonrise and moonset on the horizon.

The High Priest accepted the report and put a senior priest-administrator in charge of an expedition to explore the possibility of setting up a satellite observatory at a northern latitude. He told him to look for a site on the line of latitude 51° 50′ North, the angle of the Great Pyramid whose secant is the sacred number *phi*. An observatory at this latitude, he reckoned, would increase the accuracy of lunar observations by a factor of 3 compared with Heliopolis.

An ancient map, inherited like the eclipse records from the pre-Flood civilization of the Euphrates, marked the existence of an island off the north-west coast of the European continent at about the right latitude. The survey expedition accordingly set out to reconnoitre the coast of Britain. It was a fine summer. Proceeding west and north round Land's End, the party crossed the Bristol Channel to Wales (which they mistook for Ireland) and found that the upper reaches of the sheltered waters of Milford Haven brought them within a few miles of their objective. But the search for a site was not easy because the hinterland was covered by thick forests. Eventually, a site was found which the leader decided adequately met the main requirements: it provided a panoramic view in all directions; it was accessible from the sea; and it was located at nearly the correct latitude. [1]

After a short stay the survey party returned home and gave a favourable report to the Chief Astronomer. Plans were drawn up at once for the new observatory. It was to be a dual-purpose building, serving the needs of scientific observation and research for the priests, and of ritual ceremonies for the sun god's worship by the uninitiated. The priest-administrator was given charge of the expedition that was sent out to execute the plans. This comprised several ships to carry all the personnel and equipment needed for the construction and maintenance of the observatory: technicians who had been trained in the arts of quarrying, shaping, and transporting large blocks of stone, along with the house-builders and carpenters, doctors, farmers, weavers, and others necessary for the survival of the party in a barbarian country. Women accompanied the men, and plentiful supplies of technical equipment and stores were loaded into the holds.

Arrived at their destination the party accomplished its task according to plan and the observatory was built on the selected site. For the central obelisk and the stone circle on which the design was based, gigantic blocks of 'bluestone' were hauled from the Prescelly mountains a few miles away and cut to shape with jewelled saws. Ruthless discipline was imposed by the leader to ensure that construction work continued even while the little colony was struggling desperately for its survival. Tremendous difficulties were encountered in the work, but with courage, perseverance, and resourcefulness all were successfully surmounted.

Despite these efforts the venture itself was a failure. There was one adverse factor the Egyptians had failed to reckon with: the Welsh climate. Day after day, cloud mist and rain obscured the sky and prevented the patient observers from getting more than an occasional glimpse of sun and moon at the critical points in their orbits. Month after month went by, year after year, and only the most meagre information was transmitted back to Egypt — not enough for the priests there to effect any improvement in their predictions of eclipses.

At length the priest in charge reported that his task was hopeless. There was nothing for it but to move the whole structure to a more favourable site. This time a more extensive survey was conducted not limited to coastal areas. A site was found on Salisbury Plain where the climate was drier and the horizon less broken by jagged hills. It was some distance inland, but the friendly relations that the Egyptians had established with the indigenous population had by now given them such confidence that they no longer felt their lives depended on sea communications with their homeland. The latitude of the new site was half a degree further south than the original one, but this was an advantage for their mathematical calculations because it made the cosine of the angle almost exactly 5/8 — a much easier fraction to handle than the Pyramid angle's 55/89.

The priest in charge enclosed detailed drawings of the proposed new observatory with his report. The plans were approved in Heliopolis and orders were given for the task to be begun of transporting the massive bluestones from South Wales across the Bristol Channel, up the river Avon and thence overland to Salisbury Plain.

But the priest had reckoned without the temper of his people. It was bad enough for them to have to abandon the homes they had built and the crops they had sown with so much toil and to have to start all over again in a new country. To undertake in addition the colossal task of lifting the massive stones of their temple, transporting them by land and sea and setting them up afresh on a new site was more than could be borne by any save the most dedicated believers in the sun god's power. When the priest in charge attempted to enforce his orders a group of young men mutinied. Riots ensued, in one of which the priest was killed.

He was succeeded by his second-in-command, the mathematician who had drawn up the original report on eclipse prediction. Though young and inexperienced, this man soon proved himself equal to the heavy responsibility that now fell on his shoulders. He restored order in the community and persuaded the people to move to the site chosen by his predecessor, but agreed to postpone the work of moving the temple to a later period.

Experience in Wales had shown that to site a research station in the middle of a town was a mistake. It was difficult for the priests to protect their secrets from discovery, and frequent religious ceremonies for the populace interrupted scientific work. Moreover, the smoke from hundreds of fires all round the observatory darkened the sky and hindered accurate observation of the heavens. Foreseeing that what was now a small town would one day become a great city, the young leader decided that on its new territory the settlement would be split into two parts. The town would be built some distance to the north and a new ceremonial temple erected there for the people's worship, while a temporary structure would be built for the priests on the approved site further south, whither the stones of the existing observatory would in due course be moved. By siting the town to the north he made sure that the smoke from its fires would create the least interference with the astronomers' work because that was the direction in which they would be making the fewest observations.

The move took place as planned, and the first King of England — for that is what in fact the young priest now became — built England's first city on the Marlborough Downs at Avebury, and the first observatory-temple at Stonehenge. Many years were to elapse before the community could be brought to undertake the labour of transporting the bluestones from Wales. When, eventually, that work was carried out, it was as an act of expiation for the murder of the chief priest who had been the colony's first leader. That was a crime that his successors never allowed the people to forget, for until it was expiated every misfortune that befell the community was attributed to Ra's anger on account of it.

The first king died after a reign of forty years during which he had ruled his people justly and wisely and had guided them safely through seemingly insurmountable difficulties. His subjects revered him as no other Egyptian had been revered since Imhotep. Many believed that he was, in fact, the reincarnation of that great master. The native barbarians worshipped him as a god. He was indeed a man well fitted for the role that destiny had assigned to him — to be the founder of a new civilization in the West. Such was his greatness in the eyes of all his people that they buried him with honours which in his own country were reserved for the divine Pharaoh alone. They embalmed his body and buried it with his personal treasures deep underground, and over his grave they raised a Pyramid. That Pyramid is known to-day as Silbury Hill.

Notes on Chapter 11

1) The site which we tentatively suggest may have been chosen for the original observatory — 'Stonehenge 0' one might call it — is on a hill overlooking the estuary of the river Towy in Carmarthen Bay. The place is on the west side of the river, and is marked 'Myrddin's Quoit' on the 1-inch Ordnance Survey map. It is suitably open with an all round view — though the skyline, as anywhere in Wales, is far from level. It is at about the right latitude, and — most important — was easily accessible by sea. But despite the name there is no sign today of any stone circle. Only an electricity pylon stands on the spot where an Egyptian obelisk may once have stood, signifying symbolically the arrival of a new technological age.

12 The Message of the Megaliths

SO LONG as the Old Kingdom of Egypt lasted and the great priesthood of Ra-Harakhte continued to hold sway over the Egyptian people, the little colony in Britain remained in continuous contact with the parent observatory at Heliopolis, receiving supplies of technical equipment, paper and medicines in exchange for accurate astronomical data regarding the motions of the sun, moon and planets. But there came a day when a ship arrived from the Nile bringing no supplies but filled instead with refugees from the bloody massacres of the Egyptian revolution which, in a sudden outburst, had liquidated the priesthood and destroyed the records of their secret lore. No further communication was henceforth possible between Egypt and Britain. Avebury and Stonehenge were left to fend for themselves.

Their new isolation forced a number of changes in the British Egyptians' way of life. Being now entirely dependent on local resources for everything they needed and being unable to remit their redundant population back to Egypt as their numbers grew, they fanned out from their settlements to occupy large tracts of country further afield. While Avebury remained the administrative capital, Stonehenge grew in importance as a centre of education and culture for the expanding population. Near it there grew up a town in and around which were located a training centre for the education of young priests, a stadium for their physical exercise, and an enlarged establishment for scientific research. Priority continued to be accorded to astronomical studies because the prediction of eclipses provided vital means of impressing the native barbarians; but increasing importance was now attached to more practical forms of magic, notably medicine. In this field over the course of centuries the priests built up a fund of knowledge and skill which they applied with such effect throughout the country that the people of Britain became proverbial in other lands for their health.

To their own community the priests taught the religious doctrine on which their technical civilization was founded: the

160

creation of the Universe by a divine Intelligence, personified as the sun god, and the inevitability of divine justice for all men through the process of reincarnation; for death, they said, is but a temporary interval in the cycle of eternal life.

Underlying this belief was a mathematical secret which had been handed down as part of the ancient wisdom from priest to priest in continuous succession from the founder of the first civilization. The clue to its nature is to be found in the science of astronomy. Those ancient astronomers, wiser than the men of today, studied the forms of life on earth as well as the motions of the heavenly bodies, and they drew comparisons. They noted how life begins as a tiny speck, waxes in size and strength from birth through infancy and adolescence until it attains its full maturity, and then wanes, shrivelling and weakening through old age to death.

Just like the phases of the moon.

From their studies of eclipses those men discovered that what changes in those changing phases is not the moon itself, as everyone had thought, but only the moon's light which it receives and reflects from the sun. By making calculations and checking them against observations they established the fact that the moon is a solid sphere, and the reason why it appears to wax and wane is that the velocities and angles of its orbit round the earth are different from those of the earth's orbit round the sun. Could it not be, then, that creatures that live and die are like the moon, and that the lives they appear to live on earth, waxing and waning, are not their real selves but merely reflections of the conjunctions of those selves with the physical forces of the earth? In that case a man's real self or soul is a solid body which is fully manifest only when his life is at the full, that is to say when he is at the height of his powers midway between birth and natural death. In childhood and old age his light is less not because his soul is less but because the angle of inclination between it and the earth's orbit makes it appear less.

Even when the moon is at the full the light that it sheds upon the earth comes only from its surface. The solid sphere beneath the surface is invisible. So the body of the human soul, however bright the light with which it shines, is itself invisible.

But how could the soul be described as a 'solid body' or as 'having a body' if it cannot be seen or touched? And where is it when the physical body that it animated on earth is dead and buried? To these questions posed by the analogy of astronomy

161

the same analogy suggested an answer. The earth moves only in the plane of the ecliptic; but the moon moves round the earth in a plane which is inclined to the ecliptic in another dimension and which cuts it at two points — the ascending and the descending nodes. Might not the soul revolve similarly round the earth in higher dimensions outside the three dimensions of space, cutting the earth's orbit at the nodal points of birth and death? In the period of life that intervenes between the nodes the force of the soul mingles with the forces of the earth and forms them into the shape of the physical body that it needs for the performance of its function. As the moon's function is to reflect the light of the sun, so the function of the human soul is to reflect the light of reason that it receives from the divine Intelligence. This is why the astronomer-priests of Egypt personified that Intelligence as the sun god Ra and referred to him as 'Ra of the two horizons'.

The two horizons of Ra were the 'light horizon' and the 'life horizon'. Ra of the light horizon was the real sun in its capacity as the source of the world's material energy; Ra of the life horizon was the divine Intelligence which is the source of the spiritual energy that characterises all living things and finds its highest expression in human intelligence. The two horizons thus represented the material and the spiritual worlds, the term 'horizon' itself being a mathematical term used to denote a system of dimensions, or what a modern mathematician might call a 'frame of reference'.[1]

Ra of the life horizon was represented in Egyptian funerary art as a flattened circle or solar disc (flattened because a true circle would have involved the use of the irrational and material number *pi*) riding on the hindquarters of two lions seated back to back. Here, as in the Sphinx, the lion is symbolic of force. The lions' names were *Shu* and *Tefnet*. They represented the two primordial forces of life — forces whose names are not to be found in the vocabulary of the physicist or the chemist but which constitute the motivations of all living things — namely, *desire* and *fear*.

Shu, the force of desire, was a male god who was associated with the future, because desire is the cause of male aggressiveness and it is a force operating in the time dimension, pulling forward into the future. Shu was sometimes identified with the seminal fluid, regarded both as the source of sexual desire and as the point of entry through which all life's desires and aspirations enter the body at conception. Tefnet, the force of fear, was a wan character compared with Shu. She was a female deity associated with the past, because timidity is a feminine characteristic and fear pulls backward in the time dimension, away from the future towards the past.

36. Shu and Tefnet. *The priest Ani prays to Ra who rests on the backs of the lions Shu and Tefnet*

The two lions were portrayed sitting back to back because desire and fear pull in opposite directions. They have their forelegs straight and heads erect to show that they are independent forces with wills of their own; but their hindlegs are folded under the weight of Ra, the force of reason and self-control which holds the two lions in check. (For obvious reasons Egyptian funerary texts never represented the situation that arises when one of the lions stands up, throws Ra off his back, and gallops away — that is to say, when a person loses his self-control either in anger through frustrated desire or in panic when faced with a sudden danger.)

The human soul itself on which these forces act was portrayed by the Egyptian priests as a small, three-dimensional object with the face of the dead man and the wings and eye of Ra's son Horus. For since, they argued, the body has three dimensions co-extensive with the dimensions of the physical world, it follows that the forces which come from the spiritual world beyond the horizon of our vision to mould and animate it must act on it from a different frame of reference comprising three other dimensions which intersect transversely those in which it has its physical existence.

If it is possible to calculate the lunar orbit and measure its angle of inclination to the ecliptic, might it not also be possible to calculate the orbit of the soul as it proceeds from life to life in those non-spatial dimensions? The astronomers considered how this might be done. Here they noted an important difference between the moon and the soul. The moon is an inanimate object revolving round and round for ever along the same immutable path and never changing. Its path is a circular one, governed by the irrational number *pi* which is the number of eternal sameness. But the soul is a living thing, for ever moving and growing and developing. Life abhors circles but it delights in evolving spirals and in five-fold symmetry, and the direction of its evolution is towards increasing rationality. Surely then, the soul's progress is not a repeating arithmetical sequence governed by *pi* but an expanding geometric progression governed by *phi*, in which that number multiplies itself at successive turns as it moves outwards from the irrational $\sqrt{5}$ to the higher rational numbers of the Fibonacci series.[2]

Believing this to be a true picture of the mathematical relation between the soul and the earth, or between mind and body, the astronomers calculated that the nodal points of birth and death where the infinitely small particles of the soul's 'body' make their first and last contacts with earthly matter would be the two points where powers of *phi* coincide most nearly with fractions of *pi*, namely the two approximate equations referred to in chapter 9:

$$\frac{1}{4}\pi \simeq \emptyset^{-\frac{1}{2}}, \text{ and } \frac{5}{6}\pi \simeq \emptyset^2$$

The first of these equations had been enshrined in a kind of architectural code in the massive masonry of the Great Pyramid. That edifice was a mausoleum built to entomb a dead body, and its designers were concerned to symbolise in its geometry only that part of the life cycle which contains the 'ascending node' of death. In the dying civilization of the Old Kingdom, death and how to survive it were the principal preoccupations of priests and people alike. But here in their new life in Britain the exiled colonists were liberated from that obsession and they felt an urge to dwell instead on the opposite part of the cycle, the 'descending node', where the soul is born anew into another life.

The revolution in Egypt had made the priests of Ra in Britain conscious of the great burden of responsibility they were now carrying as sole inheritors of the ancient wisdom. They alone knew, or thought they knew, the secret of immortality; and they feared that, remote and exposed to dangers as they were, the time would come when they too, would be eliminated and the secret lost. Once lost would it ever again be found? They had long since given up hope that Atum, the Founder of Civilization and Author of the ancient wisdom, would himself return to earth. (He was now known as Atum-Ra because they believed his soul, being perfect, had been reunited with the Divine Intelligence whence it came, just as the souls of the dead Pharaohs were popularly supposed to have joined Ra in his boat of millions of years.) If the Author never returned, who else could discover the secret if it were lost?

As the population of the world grew and the frontiers of civilization expanded, so, the priests foresaw, the quality of life would decline until a nadir was reached. Thereafter many centuries would elapse before civilization again attained the level of knowledge and understanding that had been attained in their own society. That would be the time for the secret to be re-discovered. Somehow, they decided, it had to be preserved and handed down across the centuries in a message which they themselves would be able to decipher when they returned in some future incarnation.

Half the message had already been incorporated in the Pyramid. They had no doubt that there it would endure and in due course be found; but without the other half it would be meaningless. The problem that they therefore set themselves to solve was how to encypher the second half so that it would be read with the first and convey the whole secret when the time was ripe.

The leaders of the British community cast about them for an idea: they wanted to devise a new form of construction which would be as durable as the Pyramid but would symbolise birth rather than death, and in which they could incorporate the mathematical equation of the descending node.

It was their own observatory at Stonehenge that gave them the idea they were seeking: a ring of stones spaced apart and open to the sky. It was the exact antithesis of the pyramidal structure. The pyramid was massively solid, square, and closed; the stone ring was light, round, and open, and it made an excellent symbol of the cycle of rebirth. Open rings were admittedly not as durable as pyramids, but this difficulty would be met by using the biggest possible stones for their construction and making so many of them that enough would be sure to survive to convey the message.

They accordingly made rings of many different shapes and sizes, some nearly circular to represent the *pi* orbit of the earth, some egg-shaped because the egg was symbolic of birth, and others flattened so as to incorporate the equation of the descending node in their geometry. Pythagorean triangles, Fibonacci numbers, and integral ratios containing the number 5 were all used to depict the *phi* orbit of the soul and to provide clues that would help in deciphering the message. They even introduced a new unit of measurement in order that every part of the construction might embody the number $\sqrt{5}$ which their ancient lore ascribed to the life force itself.

The rings were laid out with the same meticulous accuracy as had been used in the building of the Pyramid, and megaliths were aligned with the risings and settings of sun moon or stars in such a way that they could be used for the accurate measurement of the seasons and for the prediction of eclipses. The lunar observatories served two purposes, one practical, the other symbolic. In the first place it was necessary for the priests of Ra to be able to predict eclipses in order to impress the uninitiated, particularly the native barbarians, with the Britons' power to influence the sun god, and the more observatories they had the better were their chances of observing the lunar maxima. But the more important purpose of the observatories lay in their symbolism. It was the technique of predicting solar eclipses from lunar observations — a technique that had been pioneered in Britain — that had first provided positive proof that the waning moon was a solid body which continued to exist when it was no longer visible; and it was therefore this technique that provided for the astronomers a kind of symbolic proof that a man's soul, too, continues to exist after his life has waned and flickered out from his body in death.

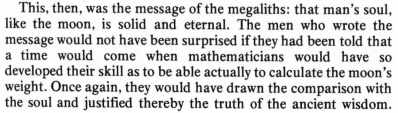

This, then, was the message of the megaliths: that man's soul, like the moon, is solid and eternal. The men who wrote the message would not have been surprised if they had been told that a time would come when mathematicians would have so developed their skill as to be able actually to calculate the moon's weight. Once again, they would have drawn the comparison with the soul and justified thereby the truth of the ancient wisdom.

The soul too, they would have said, has weight. Is it not an obvious fact that some men's personalities are weightier than others? Massive characters keep a steady course in the roughest storms, whilst the light and fickle are blown this way and that by every changing breeze. Is not this fact just as real as the fact that grain is heavier than chaff? This was the reason why every Egyptian child was brought up to believe that when he died the funeral god Anubis would take his soul and place it in the scales for Thoth the scribe to record its weight. That weight was proportional to the preponderance of good deeds over bad that he had committed in the course of this and former lives. According to which way the balance tipped, rewards or punishments would be meted out to him by the Judge Osiris.

If the priests had been told that in a still later generation men would subject their theory of the moon's solidity to its final acid test by actually walking on it and bringing pieces of it back to earth, the astronomer priests might then indeed have been surprised; but again they might have pointed a moral. Is this not an indication, they might have said, that the time is near when final proof will be given of man's immortality through physical contact with the reincarnate souls of the dead? When mathematicians can compute a course to the moon, will they not also be able to compute the orbit of a man's soul and predict the time and place of his rebirth? Like the planets, the weightiest souls of the historical past will surely be identifiable, when they return, by the characteristic qualities of the light they shed.

It is an interesting coincidence, if nothing more, that the rockets from which the first landings on the moon were made were named after the ancient sun god APOLLO.

Notes on Chapter 12

1) This interpretation of the term 'horizon' as a system of dimensions would explain the inscription in the Great Pyramid which reads 'the light horizon of Khufu (Cheops)', meaning that it was the tomb of that Pharaoh's body. The fact that the Pyramid also has meaning in relation to the Pharaoh's soul is indicated by its dedication to Khnum the god of life and arbiter of the 'life horizon'. See A. Pochan, *L'Enigme de la Grand Pyramide* (Robert Laffont, Paris 1971, p. 18).

2) See note 8 to chapter 9 (p. 137) for Schwaller de Lubicz' description of the Golden Number as constituting for the Egyptians something more than just an ideal proportion. It was a philosophical

concept in itself. *Phi*, the irrational number that eventually attains rationality, was held to link the physical with the metaphysical or spiritual world and so to be the very 'stuff' of life, which spans the two.

13 A Waxing and a Waning

THE LOCAL inhabitants whom the Egyptians first encountered in Britain were gentle people, few in numbers. As time passed, waves of barbarians of other races, each more aggressive than the last, invaded the country from the east and south. The Egyptian settlers were not warlike people and it was contrary to their religion as well as to their nature to offer armed resistance to an enemy. When the time came, therefore, that a wild barbarian horde armed with daggers and battle-axes burst upon the cities of the Egyptians, they found those cities undefended. Seized by hatred of this higher form of life which they did not understand, the barbarians sacked and burned the cities and slaughtered the inhabitants as they prayed in vain to the sun god to save them. Only the community of priests at Stonehenge escaped intact. Awed by demonstrations of magic and fearful of the supernatural power that the priests could command, the barbarians left them alone.

In the course of time a kind of civilization returned as the invaders grouped themselves in settled communities and mixed with the scattered remnants of the Egyptian population. This was the so-called 'Wessex culture' of warrior kings and powerful nobles. The priests at Stonehenge remained aloof. They established formal relations with the new rulers but took care to retain their status as a separate alien caste of priest-magicians so that they could preserve their secrets inviolate.

Theirs was a lonely life of constant peril without means of communication with other civilized communities. The seas were infested with pirates who made regular communications impossible, and such attempts as were made to establish contact with the government of the Middle Kingdom met with no response. Amon had succeeded the sun god as chief national deity; his priests were not interested in metaphysics; and the Pharaoh, dictator of the socialist state that was proud of having destroyed the religion of the Old Kingdom, regarded these exiled descendants of the pre-revolutionary priesthood as enemies of the people. When the Middle Kingdom in its turn succumbed to the domination of the alien Hyksos kings, Egypt was even further cut off from England and it seemed that the last link between the two lands had been broken for ever. The colonists thought of themselves no more as Egyptians but as Britons, calling themselves 'Abaridons' after the name of their city Abaris or Avaris, which is today called Avebury.

37. The Lions of Delos. *These archaic lions near the temple of Apollo on Delos date from the 7th century BC. Note the resemblance to Shu and Tefnet (fig. 36)*

At last a joyful day came when contact with civilization was once more established. A ship sailed into the sheltered waters of what is now the port of Southampton, and from it stepped ashore men who were very far from being barbarians. They were a band of priest-scientists from Delos, come on a voyage of exploration that had been organised by the church of Apollo, Greek-born god of healing and of the arts and sciences.

The freemasonry that had existed among priesthoods since the Old Stone Age was such that the newcomers at once recognised the priests of the Egyptian sun god for the men of science that they were. A friendly rapport was established between them, gifts were exchanged, and arrangements were made for future collaboration. The Delians were impressed with the Britons' knowledge of medicine which, thanks to generations of patient research, was far in advance of their own. Nor were they slow to recognise the advantages of having at their disposal a scientific research station far removed from the prying eyes of their inquisitive fellow-countrymen, where nature's secrets could be prised open privily and put to service for the glorification and enrichment of their god.

Already wealthy from the proceeds of the Delphic oracle, they now invested large sums of money in rebuilding and re-equipping the dilapidated structure of the Stonehenge buildings. The old double circle of bluestones that had replaced the original wooden supports for the observation platform (which had long since become dangerous and been removed) was dismantled and a new circle built with freshly quarried stones even bigger than the original. The place now was less of an observatory and more a place of worship for the uninitiated among the growing population of the town that now adjoined it. But the Britons still had use for accurate astronomical observations and they were careful, therefore, to preserve the original astronomical sight-lines wherever they could.

The research laboratories were housed in a separate compound in the town some distance from the stone circle, and these the Delians enlarged. They were confident of securing a good return on their investment in the form of medicines and medical supplies of unique excellence exported annually from Britain to Greece. Two changes, however, they insisted on as conditions of their support of the Stonehenge temple. One was that the name of the god to whom it was dedicated should be changed from Ra to 'Hyperborean Apollo'. The other was that women should be given equal status with men in the priesthood, because their own priesthood had been founded and was still controlled by women. Since only women were admitted to their most arcane rites, they insisted that only girls should be employed as messengers to carry the secret medicines to their temple in Delos. (These were the precious 'offerings packed in wheat-straw' which were referred to by Herodotus.) [1]

171

This was the high point in the history of Stonehenge. At no other time, before or after, did the Britons there enjoy a higher standard of prosperity. But those halcyon days did not last. There came an evil day when a barbarian chief, jealous of this display of wealth by people who refused him their allegiance, attacked the town, set fire to its buildings, and put its inhabitants to the sword. The laboratories and the accumulated results of generations of patient work were totally destroyed. Only the stone circle and those who took refuge in its sacred precinct escaped.

After this disaster the Delian priests conceived the idea of rebuilding the laboratories inside the stone circle where they would be protected by the aura of sacred mystery attaching to the stones. By raising the building up on stilts over the stones they could still retain the astronomical sight lines and at the same time provide cover for the stones against erosion by the elements. A grand architectural design was accordingly prepared. A wide wooden structure supported on stout oak pillars was erected in a circle outside the outer ring of stones. On this as foundation a wooden dome was constructed over the whole area, and a floor was suspended from the dome which provided enough space to house all the research workers and their precious equipment.

For hundreds of years this mighty hemispherical structure dominated the landscape of southern England; but its remoteness from civilized lands prevented it from acquiring the fame it might otherwise have justly claimed as one of the wonders of the world. Outside the priesthood it had been seen only by a few adventurous travellers, none of whom knew the work that was done there. Nor were its secrets ever divulged — save once to one man only in the last days of its existence.

The kings of Minoan Crete and Mycenaean Greece came and went. The Wessex culture of Britain and the Bronze Age civilization of the Mediterranean collapsed into anarchy; and the new Iron Age culture of the Greco-Roman world sprouted from their ashes. Throughout the dark ages of the early centuries of the first millennium BC, the priests of the Olympian gods continued to support themselves and their religion on the irrational fears and superstitions of the people. And throughout this time the temple of Hyperborean Apollo, like the remote monasteries of Scotland and Ireland in the Dark Ages of Christendom, kept alight the torch of reason and knowledge.

By the sixth century BC the wooden dome of the temple was so old that ordinary maintenance work no longer sufficed to preserve it. The great oak beams and their supporting pillars were attacked by vermin and the roof was threatening to cave in. A detailed survey showed that the building was unsafe. Moreover many of the stones underneath, despite their being protected from the weather, were leaning dangerously. Nothing less than the complete reconstruction of the dome and the under-pinning and re-erection of many of the stones was necessary to ensure that the building would continue to stand up.

But the church in Britain was poor. Contact with Delos had been lost and no other source of revenue had been found to replace it. Without a large supply of gold the labour for the work could not be obtained. There was only one thing to do: to make a public appeal for funds. The hereditary chief priest and current holder of the name Abaris accordingly set out on a tour of the civilized world to collect gold for his decaying temple.

Although most people had now heard of the marvellous hemispherical temple of Hyperborean Apollo, Abaris did not rely solely on its fame, nor on the fabulous reputation of its god, to elicit voluntary contributions towards its preservation. Like all priests of the ancient world, the main argument he relied on to persuade people of the power of his god to grant their prayers, and hence of the god's worthiness to receive their money, consisted in exhibitions of magic.

It so happened that this Abaris was a technician of exceptional brilliance who had recently brought to a successful conclusion a long programme of research and development work aimed at producing prophylactics against certain diseases which rendered large areas of Europe, then covered by swamps, uninhabitable by man. The priest-scientists had developed various kinds of serum which afforded protection against these diseases, of which the commonest was malaria. The triumph of Abaris himself was his invention of a hypodermic needle by means of which the serum could be injected into the blood.

Armed with this needle, which was to become famous as his 'magic dart', and quantities of serum, Abaris and his colleagues set out on their mission. They travelled overland, passing safely across many tracts of uninhabited mosquito-infested country which were universally regarded as impassable. It was generally supposed that the food that grew there was poisonous. When asked how he had managed to survive in these regions Abaris showed his 'dart' and let it be inferred that by means of its magic properties he was enabled to fly through the air without having to touch the disease-ridden ground or eat the noxious food. In consequence of this he became known as Abaris 'aerobates', 'the walker on air'. His fame as a magician preceded him and large crowds gathered to see him when he arrived in Greek cities. Wherever he went he performed miracles of healing. In one town he even halted a general epidemic by inoculating a large section of the population with his hypodermic needle.

All the money that Abaris succeeded in obtaining in Greece was still far from enough for his purpose, so he decided to pursue his mission in Italy.

After visiting Sybaris, the wealthiest of all the wealthy cities in that country, Abaris went on to the neighbouring city of Croton where he observed an extraordinary contrast. Whereas the Sybarites were wholly engrossed in the pursuit of pleasure and were a by-word even in Italy for their dissolute morals and their luxurious way of living, the Crotoniats lived modest, frugal lives, worshipping their gods, spurning material wealth and pursuing aesthetic pleasures such as poetry, music and dancing. The difference was due to one man, a miracle-worker of even greater fame than Abaris, a man who was believed by many to be a demi-god, whose moral teaching had influenced the whole economy of the city of Croton and who was now in effective political control of its affairs. Abaris lost no time in seeking him out. He in turn, having, when in Delos, studied the plans of the temple of Hyperborean Apollo, was no less eager to meet its renowned master-magician.

The meeting of the Briton Abaris with Pythagoras of Samos must be reckoned amongst the great encounters of history. These two men of intellect surpassed all others in their knowledge of science, religion, and mathematics; and both alike concealed their knowledge from public view under a cloak of supernatural mystery. The Master of Samos, so Abaris heard, was of divine origin and said to be in direct communication with the god Apollo. Like himself, he had the reputation of being able to fly through the air, for it was fabled that he had appeared in two widely separated places at the same time. But his most renowned feature, which proved him to be no ordinary mortal, was his golden thigh.

There was no need for either man to undeceive the other as to his true nature. Pythagoras treated his guest to a demonstraton of how an ingenious mixture of gold dust and olive oil gave any part of the human body to which it was applied the appearance of being made of solid gold. Abaris in return demonstrated the principle of his hypodermic needle. But it was in conversing on matters more profound than these trifling deceptions — the stock-in-trade of all ancient priesthoods — that the two men's true community of intellect was discovered. The priest of Hyperborean Apollo, whose knowledge of the mathematical doctrine of rebirth had been inherited from his predecessors in the priesthood, was astounded to find that the Greek had acquired this same knowledge for himself from studies in Egypt and Chaldaea although the secret had long since been lost in those countries. Pythagoras had in fact already taught his own version of the geometry of reincarnation to a select brotherhood of followers whom he called his 'mathematici'. This teaching he adjured them to keep secret. To those who could not comprehend the mathematics he taught the moral principles which were derived therefrom, under cover of religious instruction. It was this teaching that was responsible for the reformation that Abaris had noticed in the people's behaviour in Croton, for they were now more concerned with grooming their minds and bodies for a satisfactory entry into their next lives than with enjoying, at the cost of such entry, the material pleasures of the present.

Abaris was so profoundly impressed by the Samian's vast knowledge, kindly personality, and unique achievements that he decided to remain in Croton. He made Pythagoras a gift of his most precious possession: his hypodermic needle. At last, he thought, he had reached his journey's end. Here was a man who was founding a new civilization based on goodness, reason, and justice. Already his 'mathematici' were governing one great city in accordance with the principle of brotherly love. The doctrine was spreading, and other Pythagorean brotherhoods would soon be gaining control of other cities. What need, then, to keep the secret of the ancient wisdom alive in his remote sanctuary in Britain? Let the temple of Hyperborean Apollo fall down. The money he had collected could be better used promoting the spread of truth in this dazzling new civilization in the south.

So Abaris remained in Croton and sent word to the priests in Britain to abandon their temple and to come out and join him. He told them, and he announced publicly, what he sincerely believed: that in the person of Pythagoras he recognised the very incarnation of his god Apollo; for he identified Pythagoras, the re-discoverer of the ancient wisdom, with Atum its Author, and Atum's light was the pure reflection of the light of Ra of the life horizon, who was Apollo.

Most of the priest-scientists who worked in the Stonehenge laboratories and were able to travel obeyed their leader and journeyed to Italy taking their books, medicines and scientific apparatus with them. Abaris and Pythagoras together installed them in a new research institute where facilities and comforts such as they had never dreamed of were put at their disposal.

A few remained behind because they distrusted Abaris' vision of an imminent Utopia. How right they were was proved not long after when the Pythagorean brotherhoods, and with them the Master himself, were massacred in popular uprisings that broke out in South Italian cities at the end of the century.

But they themselves fared little better. Not long after the scientists left, hordes of Celts (Gauls) swarmed into western Europe from the east and north, destroying civilization wherever they found it. One wave poured into Italy and all but obliterated the youthful republic of Rome. Others swept into France, Spain, and Britain. The undefended towns of the Hyperboreans were wiped out and their civilized culture disappeared almost without trace.

Some escaped the massacres by hiding in the forests. These included a number of priests who, when the invaders had settled on the land, came out of the woods and, by feats of magic and the exercise of their superior knowledge and intelligence, established themselves among the barbarians as demigods possessed of supernatural powers. They told the Celts that they were descended from the great god of thunder who by a lightning flash had impregnated an oak tree, and out of the hollow of the burnt oak was born the divine ancestor of their race. They called themselves 'Druids', which is Greek for 'children of the oak'.[2]

When the Romans came the Druids were well established as a separate priestly caste among the Celts. There was no means by which they could be identified with the Hyperboreans, and Latin historians began to wonder whether that fabulous race had ever existed. The Roman governors of Britain hated the Druids because they were masters of an occult lore of which they themselves were ignorant, and they preached a doctrine that was subversive of Roman law and order; for the Druids taught that wherever obedience to a man-made law would be in conflict with divine or natural justice it pays to defy the law, even to the point of death.

So Roman soldiers drove the Druids out of England. Some of them found refuge in the Welsh mountains. There, for another thousand years they and their descendants kept alive under the name of 'Merlin' the tradition of magic that had been passed down from father to son in unbroken succession from the time when scientists first came to Wales from Africa three thousand years before.

Then they, too, passed into oblivion. Only the Great Stones remained, the last silent memorials of a wisdom that died.

They stand there still, mysterious and inscrutable as the Sphinx, guarding their age-long secrets under the stars.

Notes on Chapter 13

1) The 'offerings' that were carried regularly to Delos from the land of the Hyperboreans are mentioned also by Pliny the Elder in the following passage. 'Nor is it possible to doubt about this (sc. Hyperborean) race, as so many authorities state that they regularly send the firstfruits of their harvests to Delos as offerings to Apollo, whom they specially worship. These offerings used to be brought by virgins, who for many years were held in veneration and hospitably entertained by the nations on the route, until because of a violation of good faith they instituted the custom of depositing their offerings at the nearest frontiers of the neighbouring people, and these of passing them on to their neighbours, and so till they finally reached Delos. Later this practice itself also passed out of use.' (Pliny, *Natural History* iv 91. Trans. H. Rackham. Loeb Classical Library.) This story is clear evidence of downward progress from a state of high civilization back to barbarism. From the fact that the Hyperboreans persevered so long in trying despite increasing difficulties and dangers to get their 'offerings' through to Delos we can safely infer that something exceedingly precious was concealed at the bottom of the packages which were addressed to the temple of Apollo and labelled, as it were, for transit purposes, *Cornsheaves Only*.

2) This story of the transformation of the remaining Egypto-Britons into Druids is intended to suggest an explanation of how the Druidic religion and culture came to possess so many features in common with those of the Egyptians and the Pythagoreans. If such a transformation did take place it no doubt occurred on both sides of the English Channel. There were few differences between the principal features of Celtic (Gallic) culture in England and France. The similarities of Druidic beliefs with those of the Eastern Mediterranean occult philosophies have been noted by many writers. W. W. Atkinson in

38. Druidic Religious Art: The Gundestrup Cauldon. *The absurdly disproportionate arms of the Celtic god upraised beside his beautifully modelled head are so similar to the upraised arms of the* ankh *in figure 39 as to suggest that the Druids cherished ancient memories of Egyptian religious symbolism*

39. Detail of the Ani Papyrus. *Isis and Nephthys worship the* djed *column.*

179

The Sphinx and the Megaliths

Reincarnation and the Law of Karma (Yogi Publication Society, 1908)
wrote:

'the ancient Druids, particularly those dwelling in ancient Gaul,
were familiar with the doctrine of Reincarnation, and believed in
its tenets. These people, generally regarded as ancient barbarians,
really possessed a philosophy of a high order, which merged into a
mystic form of religion. . . . The philosophy of the Druids bore a
remarkable resemblance to the Inner Doctrine of the Egyptians,
and their successors, the Grecian Mystics. Traces of Hermeticism
and Pythagoreanism are clearly discernible, although the
connecting link that bound them together has been lost to history
. . . Tradition has it that the original Druidic priests came to Gaul
and other countries from some far-off land, probably from Egypt
or Greece . . . They were well versed in astronomy and astrology,
and the planets had an important part in the teachings.'

Our story might also account for certain features of Celtic art, such
as their fondness for non-circular curves, which would be supposed to
characterise the geometry of the spiritual world, and their rejection of
the material world's geometry of circles and straight lines. Their
favourite curve, the tightly coiled spiral, could be an attempt by
non-mathematical people to reproduce what the Druids' forefathers
had taught long ago, but had long since ceased to be understood, about
the expanding and diminishing *phi-spirals* of the life cycle.

Part Four Epilogue

14 A Modern Parallel

THE ORGANISATION of a scientific expedition setting out from Egypt to build an astronomical observatory in Britain was a task that must have presented some formidable problems. The expedition must have comprised some hundreds of men with their wives and families in several ships; it was bound for a land more distant than any that had yet been colonized; and it was going in pursuit of a scientific aim the true nature of which would have been known only to the few priests who were in charge of the expedition. The uninitiated would have been kept, as they always were, in carefully preserved ignorance of the priests' secrets. For them the scientific aim of the expedition would have had to be disguised as a religious aim.

The first problem that the organisers of the expedition would have had to face was therefore this: how to persuade a large number of men and women who were living in relative ease and security to leave their homes, temples, and accustomed work to set out on a hazardous voyage into the unknown with no sure prospect at the end of it, except the endurance of years of toil, hardship and danger, ending in death and burial far from their native land. We shall never know just how this problem was solved; but perhaps a clue to the manner of its solution may be obtained from considering the case of another migration that took place only 140 years ago in the course of the colonization of North America.

At a time when the vast territory that lies between the Missouri River and the coast of California was virtually uninhabited except by Red Indians, a band of two thousand men, women and children set out with their flocks and herds and all their belongings to travel westwards to a promised land and to found a new civilized society a thousand miles beyond the frontier of the old. The force that held them together and spurred them on was religious faith, fortified and directed with consummate artistry by their masterful leader, Brigham Young.

The faith that inspired and still inspires the Mormon Church of Jesus Christ of Latter-day Saints was engendered by a book written by Joseph Smith, an ill-educated young man with a fertile imagination who was described by one of his contemporaries as 'a romancer of the first water'. The circumstances under which Smith came to write the Book of Mormon are described in the book's preface. An angel named Moroni appeared to him and instructed him how to find some gold plates hidden in the ground, on which was inscribed an account of how the former inhabitants of the American continent voyaged to that promised land from Jerusalem during the reign of King Zedekiah. The plates, said Joseph Smith, were engraved in 'reformed Egyptian', but he was able to translate them by the power of two stones that had been buried with them, called the Urim and Thummim. The work of translation occupied three years, with Smith speaking from behind a screen while an amanuensis wrote down his words without ever seeing the plates. Some time after the work was complete, however, considerable scepticism having been expressed as to their existence, three men were allowed to see the plates held in the hands of an angel who appeared to them as they knelt in prayer and who turned over the leaves one by one so that they could see the writing on them. Their testimony of this occurrence is printed in an appendix to the preface to the Book of Mormon.

To imply that the Mormon Church was founded on a deception carried out on a grand scale and never acknowledged is not to imply that its founder was not divinely inspired to accomplish what he did, nor to suggest that those who allowed themselves to be deceived were not genuinely obeying the divine will when they followed the commandments of their new Church. It merely places that Church on the same footing as other great religions of the world which depended for their origin on belief in miracles. Our purpose here is simply to suggest that a similar piece of deception was practised by an Egyptian priest of Ra in the third millenium BC whereby he succeeded, with the aid of an ingenious story about a Promised Land in the West, in founding another religion which established its headquarters on the chalk uplands of Salisbury Plain. There a city was founded comparable to the city which the Mormons founded by the salt-incrusted shores of the Great Salt Lake in the Rocky Mountains. From this headquarters the Egyptian colonists sent out their own colonies to populate a territory 700 miles long — north to Scotland as far as the Outer Hebrides and south to the Breton peninsular in France — just as the Mormon colonists of Salt Lake City sent out colonies to people the expanses of Utah.

Joseph Smith was martyred before the Mormons began their great trek west from their first abortive settlement on the Mississippi. That extraordinary venture was brought to its successful conclusion under the leadership of Brigham Young. Judged by his accomplishments, Young must be ranked high in the short list of the world's great leaders. He has been described, somewhat flamboyantly, as a man who combined in himself the outstanding qualities of Moses, Cromwell, Machiavelli and Napoleon.

Just such qualities must have been needed in the man who led the first colony of civilized people to Britain. They included resourcefulness in coping with practical difficulties, shrewdness in judging character, perseverance to overcome obstacles, courage in face of danger, sternness in the maintenance of discipline, justice in the settlement of disputes, humanity and generosity in dealing with natives, and above all unshakeable confidence in the rightness of the cause to which his mission was dedicated.

It is pertinent to ask here whence do great men derive the qualities of personality and intelligence that set them above their fellows. Clearly not wholly from their parents; otherwise we would have to look for the highest human qualities in our pithecine ancestors. Like other great men's parents, Brigham Young's father and mother were very ordinary people — good but indigent middle class citizens of English stock — and his ten brothers and sisters were all mediocrities. Was it then the challenge of poverty and hardship in his early youth? Undoubtedly a man's character is to some extent developed by himself as he goes through life. Qualities of leadership are developed by the act of leading. But the same difficulties that strengthen one man's character may break another's. Fire that tempers steel will melt baser metals. The question is: what is the source of those innate characteristics that make it possible to describe a man as 'a born leader' or 'a natural genius' on account of intrinsic capabilities that are manifested in him from an early age, and not in others?

The doctrine of *karma* or *psychogenic evolution* holds that a boy or girl who inherits innate talents superior to his fellows is not a random sport created by an unjust Providence but a person who is reaping the reward of efforts made by himself in a former life when he developed those very talents in the face of difficulties. The born orator, for example, is a man who laboriously and courageously taught himself the art of public speaking in an earlier incarnation. On this hypothesis the qualities that enabled Brigham Young to become the successful founder of the Mormon society after overcoming all manner of dangers and adversities must have been acquired by him as the result of heroic efforts to conduct something of the same kind of enterprise in a former existence.

The theory postulates that not only are natural talents themselves acquired in this manner, but the instinctive urges that motivate their application and their further development are also derived from the experiences of former lives. Instincts are the promptings of buried memories which recall to the subconscious mind the happy or the unhappy consequences of acts committed centuries ago, and which secretly counsel the conscious mind either to repeat, or to avoid the repetition of, similar acts in present life. On rare occasions these memories can filter through the membrane that separates the subconscious from the conscious mind, and then they may be vividly recalled. But for the most part they remain buried and can be experienced only dimly as vague and distant echoes evoked by cognate experiences of the conscious, when they may give rise to unaccountable urges or fears or to visions or revelations, or perhaps to nothing more than a curious feeling that 'this has all happened before'.

The traumatic events that must have been experienced by men and women who, in Bronze Age Egypt, were induced to put faith in a divine revelation and to set out on a voyage into the unknown to found a new society under the setting sun would surely leave an indelible mark on the moulding of those people's unconscious minds, a mark that would endure through many subsequent incarnations. Such people would therefore be instinctively stirred by the story of the similar voyage told by Joseph Smith in the Book of Mormon. And if their prehistoric adventure had produced happy memories of fresh air and freedom, then those people would be at once the most likely to become converts to the Mormon religion and the best fitted individually and collectively to carry out its obligations. In particular they would show unquestioning faith in the divinely inspired wisdom of their leader and willing acceptance of the discipline he imposed.

A number of features in the history of the Mormon society may take on a new meaning when viewed in this light. The theory might explain, for example, why the Mormons attached so much importance to the building of temples, why their temples are secret places that only initiates are allowed to enter, and why the great temple in Salt Lake City was built on such a massive scale, after the manner of Stonehenge.

The temple was designed by an architect who had studied in Europe, but its dominant features were determined by Brigham Young in accordance with a 'vision'. He said:

> 'I do know it is the duty of this people to commence to build a temple. Now some will want to know what kind of building it will be. Wait patiently, brethren, until it is done and put forth your hands willingly to finish it. I know what it will be. I scarcely ever say much about revelations, or visions, but suffice it to say, 5 years ago last July I was here, and saw in the spirit the temple not ten feet from where we have laid the chief corner stone. I have not inquired what kind of a temple we should build. Why? Because it was represented before me. Wait until it is done. I will say, however, that it will have six towers to begin with, instead of one.'[1]

Six is an unusual number of towers to find on a rectangular edifice. Even though they are grouped in two groups of three at either end of the building and the centre tower in each group is bigger than the ones that flank it, the arrangement still offends the canons of good architectural design. But six would be an entirely suitable number for a circular building. In the centre of Stonehenge III there are five massive trilithons arranged in a horseshoe pattern, and the one in the centre is bigger than the others. We have already given reasons for believing that in the original 'Stonehenge 0' in Wales there may have been an inner sanctum of six trilithons, of which the two facing the midwinter sunset and the midsummer sunrise opposite were bigger than the other four. Could the Mormon leader's 'revelation' or 'vision' have been a distant vision of that imposing structure, recollected from four thousand years ago?

Brigham Young and his Mormons thought they were building for eternity. The six-foot walls of their temple are made of gigantic blocks of granite cut from a mountain some twelve miles away. Each block had to be carried separately on a wagon hauled by a team of oxen. Though the journey lay across a waterless

(*over*) 40. The Mormon Temple. *Behind the temple can be seen the domed roof of the Mormon tabernacle.*

plain it was proposed at first to carry the blocks by water. A canal was dug for this purpose, but abandoned when the method was found to be impracticable. The idea of water transport no doubt arose from recent memories of the convenient use of that mode on the Mississippi; but is it not possible that those memories, which proved stronger than rational calculation, were fortified by a distant echo of the memory of how those massive bluestones quarried in the Prescelly mountains were carried on rafts from Milford Haven to the Towy or across the Bristol Channel to Stonehenge?

The plan of the Mormon temple is a rectangle 200 x 100 feet. Compare this with the presumed 100 Rc height of the Aubrey hole triangle and the actual 20 x 10 Rc rectangle of the King's Chamber in the Great Pyramid. On its ground floor the temple contains four chambers which symbolise four different states of world evolution. 'One large room represents the primeval world, or world as it was in the formless and vague beginning; another the Eden of Adam and Eve; another represents the world as we know it with its imperfections; while still another represents the celestial world, or life as it is to be for those who learn and properly execute the lessons of this world.'[2] In the Great Pyramid there are also four chambers, but at different levels. The highest is the perfect 'King's Chamber'. Below it is the imperfectly finished 'Queen's Chamber'. (Neither of those titles is apt.) Hewn out of the rock beneath the Pyramid is the burial chamber, and below that is a pit. The symbolism of this arrangement would seem to be closely analogous to that of the Mormon temple.

Reference has already been made to the vast wooden dome, built entirely without metal, that roofs the Mormon Tabernacle. Could its construction have been inspired by a dim recollection of how the same people, in another incarnation some centuries later, had built a dome over what had then become the Temple of Hyberborean Apollo?

It will take a great many improbable coincidences to induce in a healthily sceptical mind a presumption of the existence of a causal relation between the events that accompanied the founding of the Mormon State and those that led to the building of Stonehenge four or five thousand years earlier. Considering the extremely tenuous nature of our knowledge of the latter events it is unlikely that enough such coincidences will ever be established to prove the connection beyond reasonable doubt, even though mathematically each coincidence does not just add to the probability but multiplies it. But there is one last point of correspondence that may be worth mentioning. This is the visual similarity that exists between the white chalk uplands of Salisbury Plain and the white margins of the salt lakes that repose in the Great Basin of the Wasatch mountains of Utah.

It is recorded that Brigham Young was personally in charge of the advance party that travelled the last stage westward from the Missouri in search of a site where the Mormons could establish their permanent settlement. On the day in July 1847 when the party emerged from a canyon from which the valley could be seen 'stretching twelve or fifteen miles to the shimmering whiteness of the Great Salt Lake in the distance', Young was ill with a fever. He raised himself up in his wagon and gazed silently at the scene before him. 'Yes', he said, 'this is the place. Drive on.'

Notes on Chapter 14

1) Ray B. West, *Kingdom of the Saints* (Jonathan Cape, London 1958).
2) Robert Mullen, *The Mormons* (W. H. Allen, London 1967).

Appendix 1

Extracts from *Megalithic Sites in Britain* by A. Thom.

Flattened circles

In many places flattened circles were used of two very definite types. So far thirty or so have been found but there were probably many more, some of which may yet be located.

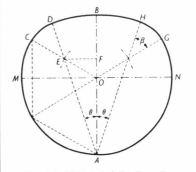 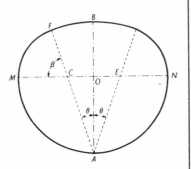

FIG. 4.1. Flattened circle. Type A.   FIG. 4.2. Flattened circle. Type B.

The construction and geometry of these rings is shown in Figs. 4.1 and 4.2. To draw a Type A ring set out a circular arc of 240° *CMANG*. The angle *COA* is easily constructed by making two equilateral triangles as shown. This makes the required 120°. Bisect *OC* at *E*. Then *E* is the centre for the arc *CD*. The remaining flat arc *DBH* is drawn with centre at *A*. To calculate π', the ratio of the perimeter to the diameter, take, for easy calculation, the radius *OC* to be 4. Then $OE = 2$ and since the angle *EOF* is 60°, $EF = \sqrt{3}$ and $OF = 1$. Also $\tan\theta = EF/FA = (\sqrt{3})/5$ which makes θ in radians equal to 0·33347. $\beta = \pi/3 - \theta$, $AE = 2\sqrt{7}$, $AB = 2 + 2\sqrt{7}$. From these we can deduce that

$$\text{perimeter}/MN = \pi' = \frac{5\pi}{6} + \frac{\sqrt{7}}{2} \times \theta = 3{\cdot}0591,$$

$$AB/MN = 0{\cdot}9114.$$

The construction of a Type B ring is easier. Divide the diameter *MN* into three equal parts at *C* and *E*. These are the centres for the small arcs. The flat

The Sphinx and the Megaliths

closing arc is, as in Type A, struck with centre at A. Making the calculations as before leads to

$$\pi' = \text{perimeter}/MN = \frac{5\pi}{6} + \frac{\sqrt{10}}{3}\theta = 2 \cdot 9572,$$

where $\qquad\qquad \tan \theta = \tfrac{1}{3},$

and $\qquad\qquad AB/MN = 0 \cdot 8604.$

We find one or two sites where a slight modification to the above types has been used. At two sites a Type A construction was used but OE was made equal to one-third of OC instead of one-half. This can be called Type D. π' for Type D is $3 \cdot 0840$ and $AB/MN = 0 \cdot 9343$. At one site Type B has been modified by making $OC = CM$. This modification makes $\pi' = 2 \cdot 8746$ and reduces the diametral ratio to $0 \cdot 8091$.

Egg-shaped rings

Ten sites are known with these peculiarly shaped rings. They can be classified into two types both of which are based on a Pythagorean or near Pythagorean triangle. In Type I (Fig. 4.3) two of these triangles are used placed base to

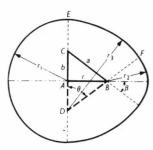

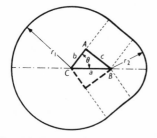

FIG. 4.3. Egg-shaped circle. Type I. FIG. 4.4. Egg-shaped circle. Type II.

base at AB. A semicircle is drawn with centre at A, an arc EF is drawn with centre at D, and the pointed end of the egg is drawn with centre at B. The result of using triangles which have all sides integral is that, provided the semicircle has an integral radius, then all the other radii must also be integral. Any given Pythagorean triangle can be used in two ways depending on which side is chosen as the base and in fact we find the 3, 4, 5 triangle turned both ways, but once the triangles are arranged the size and shape of the egg can still be varied infinitely by choosing different integers for the radius of the semicircle.

In Type II (Fig. 4.4) the triangles are placed together with a common hypotenuse. The arcs at each end are drawn with centres at the ends of this hypotenuse and joined by straight lines parallel to the side of the triangle. As in Type I if one radius is integral so is the other.

Appendix 2

Extracts from *Geometry in Egyptian Art* by Else Christie Kielland.

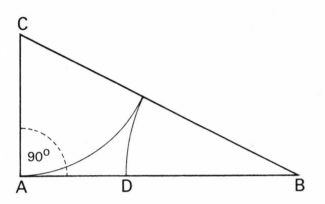

This figure shows how to divide a line AB in ϕ. The angle at A = 90°, and AC = ½AB. An arc is drawn from C through A, and an arc is drawn from B through the point of intersection of CB and the first arc. The intersection-point D then divides AB in ϕ.

Plate I-A
Plates I-A,B,C,D. HEZIRÉ. (see Fig. 9b). Circa 2750
B.C., *wood. Cairo Museum (photo: Cairo Museum).*
Analysis carried out on the basis of a photo showing the
relief on a scale equal to approximately one third of the
original. AB=82.3 cm. Main measurements checked
with the original.

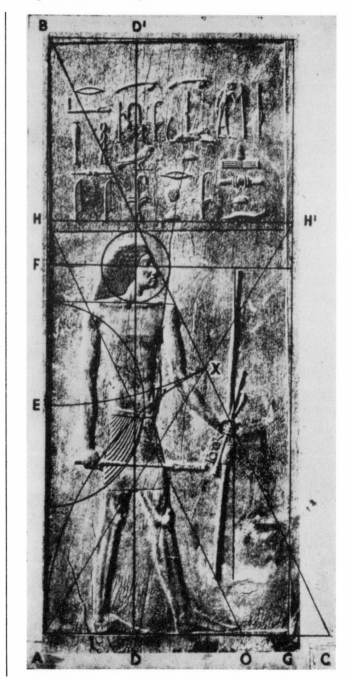

Heziré is one of the masterpieces of Egyptian art, made about 2750 B.C., showing its characteristic features fully developed. We shall start by trying to determine the geometric relationships. If we construct the $\emptyset$ right-angle ABC we at once see its importance, BC touching the forehead, nose, left shoulder and hand. An arc from C through A intersects BC at X, while an arc from B through X intersects AB at E. Point E then divides AB in $\emptyset$. H is the mid-point of EB. A line perpendicular to AB is constructed through H, and a line is drawn through A and X. As the two lines intersect at H', the base-line AG is determined.

AF = BE, which means that F is the upper point of $\emptyset$ division of AB. We can see how the staff reaches up as high as F. Its length is equal to AX, while DD', determined by BC and HH', passes through the middle of the figure marked on the straight edge of the apron. DD' is the man's vertical axis. If we imagine the man pivoting about DD' with his staff in his outstretched hand, the staff, seen from above, will describe a circle with radius equal to the distance from the staff to DD'. The diameter of this circle proves to be equal to AO ($= \frac{1}{2}$AH). We find a circle of this sort traced in about E, and it is clearly marked in the relief by the rounded edge of the pleated loin apron over the right thigh.

Appendix 3

The Geometry of the Aubrey Circle

The following geometrical construction can be used to locate, with a high degree of accuracy, 56 points at equal intervals round the circumference of a circle without first drawing the circle.

1. On a base BC, whose mid-point is P, draw a triangle ABC such that AB = AC and AP/BC = ⅝. (Figure 3.1.)

2. Bisect AB at H. Through H draw a line perpendicular to AB, and cut off HD so that DC = BC. Join DA and DB.

3. Using the same construction, bisect AC at K and erect the perpendicular KE, making BE = BC. Join EA and EC.

4. On the bases DC and BE construct two triangles DFC and BGE such that the points F and G are on the opposite side of BC from A, and the sides DF, FC, BG, GE are all equal to AB, AC. John BF, FG, GC. The figure AECGFBD is now a heptagon with all its sides and angles nearly equal.

5. Bisect FG at M, and draw MN perpendicular to FG on the side opposite to A, making MN = ¼ HD. Join FN, NG (Fig. 3.2).

6. Repeat this construction twice more, first on FN and NG and then on the hypotenuses FS, SN etc. so drawn, dividing the length of the perpendiculars by 4 each time the hypotenuses are bisected. The points at the outer ends of the perpendiculars now constitute 7 approximately equally spaced points on the arc of a circle whose circumference passes through F and G and whose centre is approximately coincident with the centre of the heptagon.

7. Repeat procedures 5 and 6 on the other 6 sides of the heptagon, thus determining, with the points of the heptagon itself, 56 approximately equally spaced points equidistant from the centre. QEF.

Note: The division of the perpendicular by 4 each time a chord (hypotenuse) is bisected is a rule of thumb which can be found empirically and which, though not exact, gives a tolerably close

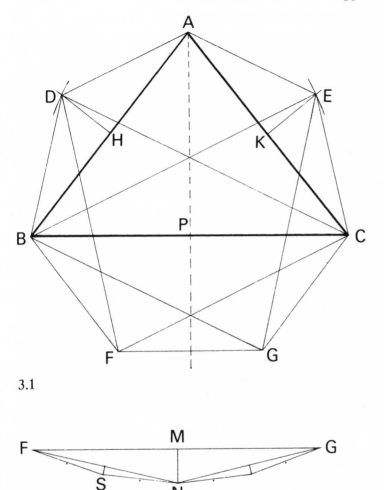

3.1

3.2

approximation to the actual value of the distance from the mid point of the chord to the circumference of a true circle. This method of drawing an arc bears some resemblance to a more complex construction, thought by Professor Thom, from the evidence of stone grids in the north of Scotland, to have been used by megalithic astronomers for extrapolating points on a space-time parabolic curve to determine the place and time of its maximum value. (*Megalithic Lunar Observatories*, p.88.)

Documentary evidence supporting the view that some method of constructing a circle from seven arcs was known to the

Egyptians is to be found in a fragment of Callimachus, the chief librarian of the great library of Alexandria (c. 250 BC). The fragment, quoted by Diodorus Siculus (x. 6. 4), refers to Pythagoras as being the first man who introduced into Greece geometrical problems 'some of which he found for himself and others which he obtained from Egypt: triangles and scalenes and the seven-lengthed circle' (*trigona kai skalena kai kyklon heptameke*). 'Scalenes' here doubtless refers to the so-called 'Pythagorean' right-angled triangles with whole-number sides, but what is a 'seven-lengthed circle'? Sir Thomas Heath in his *History of Greek Mathematics* (Vol. I p.142) thought the phrase unintelligible unless it could be taken to mean (which it surely cannot) 'the lengths of seven circles, referring to the orbits of the sun, moon, and five planets.' He was clearly unaware that a circle could be constructed in seven lengths or arcs made from triangles. Such a construction would have a natural appeal for men who had a superstitious horror of the irrational number *pi* and who wanted not to describe a perfect circle but to determine the positions of a limited number of points in a circular arrangement on the ground for a practical scientific purpose.

Index

(Page numbers shown in italics refer to illustrations.)

Abaris 95, 101-4, 170, 173-6
Abercromby, Hon J. 89
Abydos 22, 25, 30
acre 50
acusmatici 45
Adam 28, 189
Aegean 70, 71, 99
Aeneas 104
Africa 29, 55, 71, 73, 79, 80, 100, 177
Ahmose I 11
Ain Shams 23, *24*
Akhenaton 11
Alaska 54
alchemists 44
Alexander the Great 42, 43, 52, 94
Alexandria 42, 43, 49, 52
Altar Stone 81, 88
Amasis 1
Ambrosius Aurelius 62, 97
America 52, 73, 129
  Central 70, 71
  North 71, 103, 183
  South 52, 54, 55, 70
  United States of 52, 65, 129
Amon 11, 12, *21*, 169
ancient wisdom, chap. 3, 44, 51 101, 161, 165, 166, 175, 176, 177
Anglesey 88
animal worship *see* gods, animal
ankh 39, 40, *178*
Antarctica 55, *58*
anteater 32
Antigone 37

Antiquity 111-8, 121
anti-semitism 40
Anubis *20*, 25, 30-1, *31*, 48, 167
Apis 43
Apollo 36, 46, 90, 93-7, 100, 102, 167,170-1, 173-7, 189
Arabia 52
Archaic period 14
Archippus 47
Arthur, King 62
Asclepius 43
Assyrians 42
Aten 12
Athenians, Athens 40
Atkinson, Prof. R J C 65, 70, 73, 75, 78-82, 84, 86, 87, 90, 91, 92, 96
Atkinson, W W 177
Atlantic Ocean 73
Atum 15, 28, 165, 176
Aubrey holes, circle of 75, 81, 107, 111-6, 129, chap. 10, 189, App. 3
Aubrey, John 63, 75
Augustus 5, 32, 94
Avaris 104, 170
Avebury 61, 65, 87, *97*, 125, 145, 158, 160, 170
Avenue, the 78, 114
Avon, River 78, 157, 190
Aztecs 73

Babylon 42, 48, 50
Badawy, A 136
Bahia culture 73

Bardo Thodol 27
beetles 22
Bengal, Bay of 50
Berriman, A E 50, 57
bluestones 70, 78-81, 85, *86*, 87-90, 92, 140, 157-8, 171
Book of the Dead 27, *163, 179*
Boreas 94-5, 104
Brazil 71
Breton *see* Brittany
Bristol Channel 78, 156-7, 189
Brit-ain, -on, origin of name 104
Brittany 61, 66, 68, 71, 123, 184
Brutus 104
Bryn Celli Ddu 88
Buddhism 27, 43
Busiris 22

Cadmus 40
Caesars 42
Caithness 69
calculus 38
calendar 13, 56, 106
California 82, 183
Callanish 125
Callimachus 198
Cambyses 42
Cancer, tropic of 54, 57
Carmarthen Bay 159
Carnac 61, *69*, 69
Carthage 51
cartography 49, 52-6
Catalonia 51
Celts (Gauls) 48, 94, 95, 176
Cerberus 43
Chaldae-a, -ans 44, 48, 175
chambered tombs 61, 83
Cheops (Khufu) 167
    see also Great Pyramid
Chephren 13, 15
Chile 72
China 26, 50, 53, 72

Christ, -ian, -ianity 44, 116, 136, 142, 172, 183
chronometer 54, 56
cithera 94
civil service 7, 16, 34
Cleopatra 42
Cnossos 96, 102
Cohane, J P 71, 73
communism 11
computer 68, *69*, 106, 110, 115
Corinth 35, 37
cosmo-s, -logy 30, 45
Cotsworth, M. B. 91
crane 98-9
Crete 70, 90, 172
cromlech 61, 136
Cromwell 185
crook, *see* hook
Croton 103-4, 174-5
crowns, of Egypt 7, *8*
Crucuno 136
Cyclop-s, -ean 98

Daniel, Dr. Glyn 112, 116, 122
Dark Ages 80, 172
De Canario map 53
Delambre 57
Delians, Delos 48, 90, 93, 95, 99, *170*, 170-2, 173, 174, 177
Delphi, Delphic oracle 36, 37, 90, 93, 171
Delta, Nile 7, 8, 22, 104
Department of the Environment 139, 146
    see also Ministry of Public Building and Works
diffusionism 27, 73, 91
Digby, A. 149
Diodorus Siculus 91, 94, 117, 121, 200
Dionysus 29
Divine Proportion 128, 136
    see also phi ratio

djed column 39, *39, 179*
dolmen 61
dome 96, 172-3, 189
Drake Strait 55
Druids 63, 176, 177, *178*, 180
Dulcert portolano 52
dynastic race 18, 26, 30, 83
Dynasties, Egyptian
  First and Second 1, 32, 71
  Third and Fourth 8, 9, 83
  Fifth and Sixth 5, 8, 9, 10
  Eleventh and Twelfth 10
  Eighteenth to Twentieth 11, 15
  Ptolemaic 43

Earth, measurement of 49-50, 57
Easter 136
eclipse 54, 56, 68, 111, 114, 119-120, 124, 139, 153, 154-5, 161, 166
ecliptic 113, 119, 155, 162, 164
Edwards, I. E. S. 37
egg, -shaped rings 61, 123, 124, 129, 135-6, *135*, 166, 192
Egyptian Empire *see* New Kingdom
Egyptian revolution 10, 87, 160, 164
'Egyptian triangle' 129, 144, *147, 148*
Eleusis 48
Elliot Smith, Sir G. 83, 91
Emery, Prof. W. B. 5, 26
equinox 91, 95, 110
Er, myth of 48
Eratosthenes 50, 53
Er Grah 61, *62, 69*
Essenes 44
Euphrates 11, 18, 26, 27, 28, 54, 72, 156
Eve 28, 189
Eye of Horus 30, 33, 163

falcon *see* hawk
feather 31
Fibonacci series 125-31, 164, 166
  see also phi-ratio
flail 31, 38
Flood, the 26, 155, 156
force 17, 37, 162
Founder of civilization *see* Atum
frame of reference 162, 163
France 63, 72, 176
Frankfort, Prof. H. 37, 57
Frazer, Sir J. 26, 29
Freemasonry 44

Gauls *see* Celts
Genesis, Book of 28, 72
geodesy 28, 49, 50
Geoffrey of Monmouth 62, 79, 96, 104
Ghyka, Matila C. 136
Giants' Ring 63, 96
Giza *12*, 13, 129
gnosticism 44
God, gods, chap 2
  animal 17, 19, 22, *23*, 30, 33
  as intelligence 99
  Olympian 35, 36, 172
  Pythagoras' treatise on 102
  Stone Age 17, 22
Golden Dawn, Society of the 44
golden section, g. number *see phi*-ratio
Gossellin, P. F. J. 49, 50, 53, 57
Great Pyramid 13, *134*
  accuracy of 125
  as calendar 91
  as observatory 137
  as Pharaoh's tomb 13, 167
  chambers in *134*, 189
  construction of 83, 122
  geometry of 129-132, *130*, 138, 146, 156,

symbolism of 132-4, 164-5
unit of measurement in 146
Great Salt Lake 190
Greece 34, 40, 42, 43, 95, 98-9, 101-2, 171, 174
Greeks 40, 43, 48, 50, 71, 90, 93, 94, 95, 98-9, 128
grids, stone 68-9, 197
Guatemala 73
Gundestrup cauldron *173*
guru 27

Hades 29, 43
Hadji Ahmed map 52, 54
Hapgood, C. H. 51-55, 57
Harmakhis 15
Hathor 25
Hatshepsut, Queen 11, 104
Hawaiian Islands 72
hawk (falcon) 16, 19, 25, 30
Hawkes, Jacquetta 115-117, 118
Hawkins, Dr. G. S. 65, 66, 106-118, 124, 139
Heath, Sir T. 200
heaven 38, 48
Hebrides 120, 125, 184
Hecataeus 94-5
Heel Stone 75, 78, 89, 118
Heggie D. H. 122
Heliopolis 23, 24, 30, 143, 156, 157, 160
hell 29, 48
Hellenistic 44
Hengist 62
heptagon 129, 144, *148*, 149, 196-7
Hermes 42
Hermetic, Hermetism 42-4, 180
Herodotus 7, 93, 101, 171
Heyerdahl, Thor 73
Heziré *196*, 195
Hinduism 27

Hipparchus 54
hook (crook) 31, 38
Hor-aha 5
horizon 162, 167, 176
Horn, Cape 55
horseshoe, stone 88, 89, 92
Horus 16, *20*, 25-6, 29, 30, *32*, 32-4, 99, 132, 163
Hoyle, Prof Sir F. 112-4, 139
Hyksos 11, 170
Hyperboreans 93-6, 100-3, 117, 171, 176, 177

Iamblichus 48, 101-3
Iberia 48
ibis 25, 30
  see also Thoth
Imbros 48
Imhotep 9, 10, 43, 83, 159
immortality 39, 40, 165, 167
  see also reincarnation
Incas 73
India, -ans 26, 28
Indians, Red 183
Indus, River 28
Inigo Jones 63-4
initiation 34, 45
Intelligence 16, 17, 34, 37, 40, 99, 161, 162, 165
Intermediate Period, First *see* Egyptian revolution
Intermediate Period, Second *see* Hyksos
Ireland 52, 62, 79, 97, 156, 172
Iron Age 37, 101, 172
Ishtar 22
Isiac rites 137
Isis 22, 25, 26, 42, 132, 154, *179*
Israel 44
Italy 42, 46, 102, 103, 174, 176

jackal god 19, 25, 30
  see also Anubis

Jaipur 106
James I 63
Japan 73
Jehovah 44
Jocasta 35-7
Jomard, E. F. 50
Judgement, the 27, 29, *31*
Julius Caesar 63
justice 7, 27, 28, 45, 47-8, 161, 176
  see also karma

Kabbalists 44
Kalamata 99
karma 27, 28, 29-31, 38, 43, 45, 180 185
Kastro 1
Kendall, Prof. D. G. 68
Kha-Sekhemui 32
Khepri 15 *23*
Khnum 153, 167
Khufu *see* Cheops
Kielland, Else Christie 128, 193-5
Killaraus, Mount 63, 82, 97
King of England, the first 158
King's Chamber 133-4, 189
Kon-Tiki 73

Lacedemon 102
Laius 35-6
lamaism, lamas 27
Land's End 156
le Corbusier 128
Leibnitz 38
Leonardo da Vinci 128
Leto 94
life force 166
lintel 64, 81, 86
lion 15, 17, 162-3
Livingstone, Dr. 26
Lockyer, Sir N. 106, 110
locomotive 99
lunar observatories 68, 121, 166

Luxor 25, 137
Lysis 47

Ma'at 7
Macedon, -ian 42, 43
Magi 46, 48
magic 17, 33, 46, 62, 91, 96-7, 99, 160, 169, 173, 177
Mahayana 27
malaria 173
Manetho 11, 23
Manichees 44
maps 50, 51-6, 156
Maqrizi 23
Marathon 40
Marlborough Downs 61, 78, 80, 158
mask, -ed 17, 22, 33, 44
mason, -ry 86-7
mastaba 83
mathematici 46-7, 175
Mayas 73
measures, ancient 49-51, 121, *133*
  see also 'Megalithic Yard'
Méchain 57
medic-ine, -al research 79, 96, 99-103, 160, 171, 173-4
Mediterranean Sea 51, 53, 71
megaliths (Great Stones) 61-2, 115, 177
  message of the 131, chap. 12
  mystery of the, chap. 4, 152, 177
megalithic culture 51, 61, 68, 71-2, 123, 153
Megalithic Lunar Observatories 66, 121, 197
'Megalithic man' 119-121
megalithic observatories 66, 119-122, 153
megalithic sites, age of 70-1

Index

Megalithic Sites in Britain 66,
   118, 123-5, 136, 149
megalithic tombs 61, 72, 83
'Megalithic Yard' 123, 132, *133*,
   146, 149
Meggers, Betty 73
Memphis 7, 25, 31
Menes 5-8, 32
menhir 61, *62, 69*
Mercator 52, 55
meridian 54
Merlin 62-3, 79, 97, 177
Mesopotamia 72
   see also Euphrates
Metonic cycle 91, 95, 104
metric system 50, 57
metrology 50, 72
Mexico, Mexican, 71, 73, 149
Middle Kingdom 10-1, 169
Milford Haven 81, 88, 89, 156, 189
Ministry of Public Building and
   Works 115, 146
Minos, palace of 96
Minoan 34, 70, 172
miracles *see* magic
Mississippi 185, 189
Missouri 183, 190
moon
   and eclipses 119, 120, 124
   observation of, by megalithic
      people 68, 100, 124, 152
   orbit of 107, 124, 155
   phases of, like the soul 161-7
   and Stonehenge alignments
      chap. 8, *108*
   view of, from Britain 95, 121
Mormon, Book of 184
Mormons 96, chap. 14
Mormon tabernacle 96, *188*, 189
Mormon temple 187-190, *188*
Moses 44
Mycenae, -an 34, 70, 90, 99, 118,
   172

Mykerinos 13, 129
Myrddin 63
Myrddin's Quoit 159
Nalanda 27
Napoleon 49, 50
Narmer 5, 128
Nature 110, 111, 114, 121
Needham Dr. J. 53
Neoplaton-ism, -ist 44, 47, 48,
   101, 137
Nephthys 25, *179*
New Kingdom 11, 12, 128
Newall, R. S. 87, 88
Newham, C. A. 106, 114, 148
Nile *4*, 7, 8, 18, 25, 104, 153, 160
nodes, lunar 111, 113, 119, 120,
   124, 140, 162
nodes of the soul's orbit 162,
   164, 166
nomarch, nome 5, 7
Nordenskjold, A. E. 51

obelisk *24*, 91, 142, 159
observatory 24, 66, 68, 100, 153,
   156, 183
Oedipus 16, 35-7, *35*
offerings 93, 94, 171, 177
okapi 32
Old Kingdom 5-14, 25, 54, 83, 87,
   98, 155, 160, 164
Old Stone Age 17, 22
Olympus, Mt. 29
On 23
   see also Heliopolis
Orkney Islands 66
Orinoco, River 54
Orontaeus Finaeus map 55, *58*
Orpheus, Orphism 44, 48
Osiris 9, *20*, 22, 23, 25-33, 38-9,
   43-4, 48, 132, 154, 167

Pacific Ocean 52, 72

Padma Sambhava 27
Paris 50
Parthenon 57, 128
passage graves 72
Peloponnesian war 40
Pembrokeshire 78-9, 81
Periboea 35, 37
Persians 40, 42, 46
Peru 71, 73
Petrie, Sir F. 87, 91, 133, 136
Pewsey, Vale of 145, *145*
phi, phi-ratio 125-132, *126*, 137, 146, 156, 166, 168, 180, 193-5
Phoenicians 40, 50, 51, 53, 54
pi, pi-ratio 130-1, 144, 162, 164, 166
Piazzi Smyth, C. 136
Pigott, Prof. Stuart 79
Pindar 93
Piri Re'is map 52-55
place names 71-2
Plato 43, 47-8, 103, 137
Pleiades 95
Pliny the Elder 93-4, 177
Pochan, A. 37, 137, 167
Pole star 137
Polybus 35
Polycrates 1
Porphyry 47
portolano maps 51-5
Predynastic Age 8
Prescelly mountains 78, 82, 157
Proclus 137
Proctor, R. A. 137
Protestant 41
protractor 113, 140
pschent 7, *8*
psychogenic evolution 27, 38, 185
Ptah 7, *21*, 32
Ptah-Soker *see* Sakkara
Ptolemy, Claudius 49, 51
Ptolemy Soter 43

pyramids 8-10, *12*, 24, 84, 98, 165-6
see also Great Pyramid, Step Pyramid
pyramid texts 9
Pythagoras, Pythagoreans 1, 28, 43, 45-8, 101-4, 127, 174-6, 177
Pythagorean triangles 68, 124, 129, 132, 136, 144, 146, 166, 192, 200

"Q" and "R" holes 78
Queen's Chamber 189
Quiberon Bay 61

Ra, Ra-Harakhte *20*, 22, *23*, 23-5, 29-30, 40, 90, 99, 136, 163-4, 162-3, 165, 176
Rameses II 12
rebirth, reincarnation, resurrection 15, 26-9, 43, 45, 94, 134, 159, 161, 166-7, 175, 180, 186-190
Reisner, G. A. 9
remen 50, 132, *133*, 149
Republic, The, of Plato 48
riddle 16, 34-6
Rocky mountains 184
Roma, goddess 32
Roman Catholic Church 40
Rome, Romans 42, 49, 63, 104, 128, 176-7
Rosicrucians 44
Ross Sea 55
Royal cubit 132, *133*, 142, 146-9, *147*
Royal Society 66
Russia 93

Sadler, D. H. 114, 120
St Vincent, Cape 50
Sakkara 7, 9, 83

Salisbury Plain 61-2, 100, *145*, 157, 184, 190
Salt Lake City 96, 184, 187
Samos 1, 45, 48
Samothrace 48
Saros cycle 154-5
sarsen circle 64, 80-1, *148*, 149
sarsen stones 62, 64-5, 70, 78, 80-1, 87, 89-90, 99
Satan 44, 142
scarab 15, *20*
Schwaller de Lubicz 137-8, 167
Scotland 68, 118, 120, 172, 184
Scythians 93, 102, 105
semitic 72
Serapis 43-4
Seth *21*, 25-6, *32*, 32-4, 44
seven-lengthed circle 198
sexagesimal system 49, 56
shamans 17, *18*
Shepherd Kings *see* Hyksos
Shu 162-3, *163*
Siberia 54
Sicily 47, 94
Silbury Hill 61, 65, 82, *84*, 84-5, 91, 92, 159
Sinope 43
Smith, Joseph 184-5
soul 31, 161-7
Southampton 170
Spain 50, 176
see also Iberia
'spherical' 94-6, 117, 173
Sphinx *6*, 13, 15-7, 28, 34-7, *35*, 40, 162, 177
stade 49, 50, *133*
Station Stones 78, 108, 118
Step Pyramid 9, 83
stone circles and rings *60*, 61, 68, 71, *97*, 123, 130, *135*, 159, 165-6, 191-2
stone no. 36 85-7, *86*

Stonehenge *64, 66, 76*
archaeology of, chap. 5
as architecture 63-4, 85-90, 117-8
as astronomical observatory chap. 8, *108*
as burial place 98
carvings on stones of 70, 90, 99
continuity of 90, 110
dates of 81-2, 114-5
early studies of 63-4
Geoffrey of Monmouth on 62, 79
Inigo Jones on 63
latitude of 108-9, 118, 144-6, *145*
lay-out of 88, 144, *147, 148*, 148-9
Mormon temple and 187
mystery of 2, 61
old beliefs on 62
orientation of 88-9, 116
as place of healing 79
rebuilding of 90, 99, 171
roof over 96, 189
story of founding of, chap. 11
as symbol of rebirth 165
as temple 61, 63, 88, 90, 94-6, 116, 171
"Stonehenge 0" 159, 187
Stonehenge I 75-8, 81, 82, 90, 107, 115, *141*
Stonehenge II 78-80, 81, 86, 90
Stonehenge III 80-1, 87, 90, 110
Stonehenge Decoded 66, 111
Strabo 49, 57
Sumerians 49
sun, sun god, 9, 15, 23-4, 99, 161-2, 167
see also Ra, Apollo
Sybaris, Sybarites 174
Syene 54

Taygetus, Mt. 102
Tefnet 162-3, *163*
Tenasserim 50
Thebes (Egyptian) 11, 25
Thebes (Boeotian), Thebans 16, 35-6, 40
Theosophy 44
Thinae 50
Thom, Prof. A. 66-9, 118-122, 123-5, 130, 132, 144, 146, 149, 197
Thomas, Dr. H. H. 78
Thoth *21*, 25, 30, 33, 42, 43, 44, 167
Thureau-Dangin, F. 56
Thutmose III 11
Tibet 27
Timaeus, The, of Plato 47, 137
Tiryns 98
Toltecs 73
Tompkins, P. 14, 91, 137
Towy, River 159, 189
Toynbee, Sir A. 8, 23
trigonometry 28, 49, 52, 53, 54, 56, 113, 129
trilithon 64, 80, 81, 85, 87, 88, 89, 92
trinity, Osirian 132, 136
Troy 104
Turkey, Turkish 52
Tutankhamen 12
Tyre 50

ultimate incentive 38
ultimate reality 44, 46, 47
unification (of Egypt) 5, 8, 19, 23, 25, 30
Utah 184, 190

Valdivia culture 73
Viollet-le-Duc 129

Waddell, A. 37
Wales, Welsh 70, 87, 92, 100, 149, 156, 157, 158, 177
Wasatch mountains 190
weighing of souls 31, *31*, 167
Wessex, Wessex culture 70, 92, 99, 118, 169, 172
West, J. A. 138
West Indies 71
West Kennet long barrow 61
Wheeler, Sir M. 83, 91
Windmill Hill 61
witch, wizard 101
witch hunts 40
Woodhenge 124

"Y" and "Z" holes 81, 96
Yahweh 44
Yellow River 28
yoga 27
Yorkshire Post 106
Young, Brigham 183, 185, 187, 190

Zeus 43, 44
Zoroaster 46
Zoser 9, 10, 83

SCHOOLCRAFT
COLLEGE LIBRARY